I0005291

AVERY LOCKE

C++ for scalable software Architecture

Copyright © 2024 by Avery Locke

All rights reserved. No part of this publication may be reproduced, stored or transmitted in any form or by any means, electronic, mechanical, photocopying, recording, scanning, or otherwise without written permission from the publisher. It is illegal to copy this book, post it to a website, or distribute it by any other means without permission.

First edition

This book was professionally typeset on Reedsy.
Find out more at reedsy.com

Contents

Introduction : Scalable Architecture in Modern Software

Importance of Scalable Architecture in Modern Software

1. The Modern Software Landscape

The digital age has transformed how businesses and individuals interact with technology. We are witnessing an era where software isn't just a set of instructions but a driving force behind economies, healthcare, education, finance, and almost every aspect of modern life. As a result, the demand for software applications capable of handling massive user loads, enormous data sets, and complex computations has skyrocketed. This is where the concept of scalability becomes indispensable.

Scalability refers to a system's ability to handle increasing loads without compromising performance or user experience. Whether dealing with a growing number of users, increased transaction volumes, or the expansion of data processing requirements, scalability ensures that your software can grow and adapt seamlessly. Businesses that fail to embrace scalable architecture often find themselves unable to compete, as their systems struggle to meet user demands, leading to downtime, inefficiencies, and dissatisfied customers.

2. Challenges in Achieving Scalability

1

Achieving scalability is far from trivial. Developers must consider several factors, such as handling concurrent users, maintaining data consistency across distributed systems, and ensuring that the performance of key operations remains consistent. A robust software architecture provides the roadmap to addressing these challenges by laying out the structure, components, interactions, and behaviors of the software system.

Several challenges frequently arise during attempts to build scalable software:

- **Concurrency Issues**: The ability to execute multiple operations simultaneously without errors or inconsistencies.
- **Resource Management**: Efficiently managing CPU, memory, and I/O resources as the application load increases.
- **Network Latency**: Minimizing delays in data transmission when distributed across multiple systems or geographic regions.
- **Data Integrity and Consistency**: Maintaining accurate and consistent data in the face of concurrent updates and distributed transactions.

3. Why Software Architecture Matters

Software architecture provides the blueprint to build, organize, and extend an application. It dictates the system's modularity, separation of concerns, and flow of control. A well-structured architecture not only enhances scalability but also improves maintainability, flexibility, and security.

For instance, microservices architecture has gained traction as a solution for scalability and maintainability. In this paradigm, applications are broken down into smaller, independently deployable services, each focusing on a specific task. This allows for more efficient scaling, as individual services can be scaled independently based on their load demands.

Why C++? The Power and Flexibility of C++ in Large-Scale Systems

1. The Versatility of C++

C++ has long been a staple in the development of complex, high-performance software. The language's low-level memory manipulation capabilities, combined with high-level abstractions, provide the flexibility to control every aspect of system behavior. This versatility makes C++ a preferred choice for developing scalable applications in industries like gaming, finance, telecommunications, and embedded systems.

While other programming languages have risen in popularity for certain domains, C++ remains unparalleled in many scenarios where performance, memory management, and hardware control are paramount. Its ability to operate close to the metal (the hardware) while still providing features for abstraction gives it an edge when building large-scale, high-performance systems.

2. Performance Optimization

One of C++'s standout features is its unmatched performance. When dealing with scalable systems, performance often becomes the bottleneck, and C++'s control over memory management, efficient resource handling, and direct hardware interaction enables developers to squeeze the most out of the hardware. Features like smart pointers, RAII (Resource Acquisition Is Initialization), and the Standard Template Library (STL) provide the building blocks to write scalable, efficient code.

C++ supports:

- **Low-Level Access**: Giving developers fine-grained control over memory, storage, and execution, crucial in optimizing resource usage for large-scale systems.
- **Object-Oriented Programming**: Allowing clear modularity and encapsulation, which is essential for maintaining large codebases.
- **Generic Programming**: Enabling flexible code design with templates to handle various data types and operations efficiently.
- **Functional Programming Paradigms**: With lambdas and higher-order

functions, C++ now supports more functional programming paradigms, allowing for concise and expressive code.

3. Advanced Concurrency and Parallelism

Concurrency and parallelism are vital to the scalability of modern applications. C++ excels in providing powerful features for concurrent programming, enabling developers to fully leverage multi-core processors. The introduction of features like *std::thread, std::async,* and *std::future* in the C++11 standard, as well as ongoing improvements, have solidified C++'s position as a top choice for handling large-scale, multi-threaded applications.

Additionally, C++ has extensive libraries like Boost, which offers asynchronous execution and communication mechanisms. Coupled with the efficient synchronization constructs like mutexes, condition variables, and atomic operations, developers can handle concurrency challenges more effectively in C++.

4. Strong Community and Ecosystem

The C++ community is mature, with a plethora of well-tested libraries and frameworks available to solve common problems in software architecture. From Boost to Qt, and libraries like gRPC, ZeroMQ, and more, the C++ ecosystem provides robust support for networking, concurrency, cross-platform development, and more.

Furthermore, C++'s consistent evolution (with the introduction of newer standards like C++20) ensures that developers can leverage modern techniques and patterns without sacrificing backward compatibility or performance.

5. Case Studies of C++ in Large-Scale Systems

C++ has a track record of being the backbone of several large-scale, mission-critical applications. Some of the most notable examples include:

- **Game Engines**: Unreal Engine and Unity rely heavily on C++ due to its low-level capabilities and performance benefits. These engines power many AAA games and require scalability to handle massive, dynamic environments.

- **Financial Systems**: High-frequency trading platforms are often built using C++ due to its deterministic performance and low latency, which are critical in financial markets.
- **Telecommunication Systems**: Many telecom frameworks are built using C++ to manage high loads, maintain concurrency, and provide real-time data processing.

How to Use This Book

1. Structuring Your Learning

This book is structured to guide readers from the foundational principles of scalable software architecture to more advanced techniques specific to C++. You'll find that each chapter builds upon the previous one, deepening your understanding of software architecture while focusing on the unique challenges and opportunities of working in C++.

2. Navigating the Book for Maximum Benefit

If you are new to scalable architecture, it's best to read the book sequentially. Each chapter introduces concepts, patterns, and techniques incrementally, helping you grasp the essentials before diving into more complex topics. However, if you're an experienced developer looking to fill specific gaps in your knowledge, you can explore standalone chapters based on your needs. Chapters on concurrency, memory management, and performance optimization can be especially valuable for immediate reference.

Each chapter contains:

- **Conceptual Explanations**: Thorough breakdowns of architectural principles, design patterns, and modern C++ techniques.
- **Code Examples**: Real-world implementations in C++ to illustrate key points. These examples demonstrate best practices, common pitfalls, and potential solutions to scalability challenges.
- **Practical Advice**: Tips and guidelines from experienced C++ architects to help you navigate common challenges in scalable C++ development.
- **Case Studies**: Real-world examples to provide insights into architectural

decisions made in large-scale C++ projects. Each case study highlights the challenges faced, solutions adopted, and lessons learned.

3. Learning Outcomes

By the end of this book, readers will be equipped with the knowledge and tools to:

- **Design Scalable Architectures**: Understand key principles, patterns, and techniques for designing software that scales.
- **Write Efficient C++ Code**: Master modern C++ techniques for memory management, concurrency, and performance optimization.
- **Implement Real-World Patterns**: Learn how to apply architectural patterns in C++ to solve scalability challenges.
- **Handle Complex Applications**: Gain confidence in dealing with large, multi-threaded, distributed systems in C++.
- **Optimize and Maintain Software**: Develop skills to profile, optimize, and refactor C++ code for scalable systems.

4. Supplementary Resources

Throughout the book, additional resources are recommended for those seeking a deeper understanding of specific topics. These include references to documentation, open-source libraries, research papers, and further readings. A companion website provides downloadable code examples, additional case studies, and regular updates on relevant trends in C++ and software architecture.

This introductory section sets the tone for the rest of your book, establishing the importance of scalable software architecture, the power and flexibility of C++, and the structure of the book to guide readers through the journey of mastering C++ for large-scale systems. Each of these key points will help create a solid foundation that encourages readers to continue exploring the more advanced concepts and techniques discussed in later chapters.

Chapter 1: Fundamentals of Software Architecture

Introduction

I n this chapter, we will explore the core principles of software architecture that directly impact scalability, performance, and maintainability. We'll examine key architectural principles, understand the role of software architecture in enhancing these attributes, and define scalability using measurable metrics and benchmarks. Finally, we'll look at real-world examples to solidify these concepts.

1. Principles of Scalable Software Design

1.1. Separation of Concerns and Modularity

One of the most fundamental principles in scalable software design is *Separation of Concerns (SoC)*. It refers to the idea of dividing a software system into distinct sections or modules, each handling a specific aspect or concern. This principle aims to keep code organized, maintainable, and easy to scale by isolating changes within relevant modules.

In scalable systems, SoC helps mitigate risks by confining potential failures or changes to specific areas. For example, if a new feature requires a change in a single module, that change can occur without impacting the rest of the system. This modularity enables better resource allocation and eases the scaling of individual components based on specific requirements.

- **Practical Example**: A content delivery platform could divide its system into modules like video processing, user authentication, and payment management. Each of these modules can be updated and scaled independently to meet user demand.

1.2. Loose Coupling and High Cohesion

Loose coupling is a principle that minimizes dependencies between different parts of a system. When components are loosely coupled, changes in one module have minimal impact on others, reducing the risk of breaking the entire system with a single update. High cohesion, on the other hand, ensures that each component or module is focused on a specific task, making the system easier to maintain and scale.

- **Example**: In a web application, a loosely coupled architecture may involve separating the business logic, data access layer, and presentation layer. Each layer should have high cohesion, focusing on its own tasks without relying heavily on the internal workings of other layers.

1.3. Single Responsibility Principle

The *Single Responsibility Principle (SRP)* states that each component or class in a system should have only one reason to change. This principle directly impacts scalability by ensuring that changes in functionality do not have a cascading effect throughout the system. SRP complements modularity and loose coupling, making it easier to add new features or make updates without disrupting the entire system.

1.4. Scalability by Design

Designing for scalability requires a proactive approach. The architecture must be planned with future growth in mind, anticipating increased loads, new features, and evolving requirements. Here are key practices for designing scalability into the system:

- **Horizontal and Vertical Scaling**: Understanding and planning for both horizontal scaling (adding more nodes to a system) and vertical scaling (increasing the capacity of existing nodes).
- **Stateless Design**: Minimizing or eliminating dependencies on internal states allows services to handle requests independently, making it easier to distribute workloads across multiple servers.
- **Partitioning and Sharding**: Dividing a database into smaller, more manageable segments to distribute the data load.

1.5. Fault Tolerance and Resilience

Building resilient systems is an integral aspect of scalable software design. Fault tolerance focuses on anticipating and handling potential failures gracefully. This involves mechanisms like retries, circuit breakers, and redundant systems to maintain availability even under adverse conditions.

- **Example**: A distributed cloud-based e-commerce platform might use redundant data storage across different regions to ensure that users can still access the service even if one data center fails.

2. The Role of Software Architecture in Performance and Maintainability

2.1. Performance as a Key Attribute

In the context of software architecture, performance is often a primary concern. A good architecture ensures that performance remains consistent as the system scales. The architecture must facilitate efficient communication between components, optimal resource usage, and minimal latency.

- **Case Study**: In high-frequency trading systems, where every millisecond counts, C++ is often chosen for its low-level control over hardware. These systems rely heavily on optimizing every layer of the architecture to minimize latency and maximize throughput.

2.2. Maintainability Through Architecture

Software maintainability is defined as the ease with which a system can be modified to correct faults, improve performance, or adapt to a changing environment. Good software architecture supports maintainability through principles like modularity, high cohesion, and separation of concerns.

- **Design Patterns for Maintainability**: Patterns like *Factory Pattern, Observer Pattern*, and *Dependency Injection* are vital in designing maintainable systems. They allow developers to extend and modify code with minimal impact on other parts of the system.
- **Real-World Example**: Consider a large-scale application where changes in one part of the system would previously break other modules. With a shift to a microservices architecture, changes can now be isolated, reducing the cost and complexity of maintenance.

2.3. Architectural Patterns for Performance and Maintainability

Certain architectural patterns are particularly effective at enhancing performance and maintainability. Here are some key patterns:

- **Layered Architecture**: This traditional architecture separates the system into layers such as presentation, business logic, and data access, enhancing both maintainability and scalability.
- **Microservices Architecture**: It divides the application into smaller, loosely coupled services that can be deployed and scaled independently.
- **Event-Driven Architecture**: Focuses on asynchronous processing and decoupling of components, which increases flexibility and scalability.
- **CQRS (Command Query Responsibility Segregation)**: Separates read and write operations to optimize performance.

3. Defining Scalability: Metrics, Benchmarks, and Real-World Applications

3.1. Understanding Scalability

Scalability refers to a system's capacity to handle increased workload or demand without compromising its performance or stability. However, scalability isn't just about adding more resources; it involves a combination of efficient resource usage, intelligent system design, and ongoing monitoring.

- **Types of Scalability**:
- **Vertical Scalability**: Expanding the capacity of an existing node or server.
- **Horizontal Scalability**: Adding more nodes to the system to distribute the load.

3.2. Metrics for Measuring Scalability

When assessing the scalability of a software system, certain metrics are crucial. These metrics help in defining the system's current capacity and identifying areas for improvement. Here are some key metrics:

- **Latency**: The time it takes for a system to respond to a request. Low latency is crucial in high-performance applications like real-time bidding, gaming, or financial systems.

- **Throughput**: The number of operations or transactions the system can handle in a given period. High throughput is critical in systems dealing with large volumes of data or concurrent users.
- **Resource Utilization**: Monitoring how effectively the system uses CPU, memory, and other resources. High utilization without bottlenecks indicates efficient scalability.
- **Response Time**: The total time taken to complete an operation from start to finish. This is an essential measure in user-facing applications.

3.3. Establishing Benchmarks for Scalability

Benchmarks allow organizations to measure the performance and scalability of their systems under controlled conditions. The goal of benchmarking is to create a baseline that can be used to evaluate changes or improvements.

- **Key Steps in Benchmarking**:
- **Identify Critical Use Cases**: Focus on high-priority scenarios that represent the system's core functionality.
- **Simulate Real-World Load**: Use tools to simulate traffic patterns and data loads that the system is expected to handle in production.
- **Measure Key Metrics**: Record the system's behavior under varying loads to establish a baseline for comparison.
- **Identify Bottlenecks**: Analyze the results to find bottlenecks in throughput, latency, or resource usage.

3.4. Real-World Applications of Scalable Architectures

Scalability is essential across various industries, each with unique requirements and challenges. Here are a few examples:

- **E-Commerce**: Platforms like Amazon must handle millions of transactions per second, support multiple regions, and maintain data consistency. Scalability is achieved through distributed data storage, redundancy, and microservices.

- **Social Media**: Facebook, Twitter, and Instagram handle billions of daily interactions. They rely on scalable architectures with distributed data stores, caching layers, and efficient load balancing.
- **Financial Services**: Real-time trading platforms in finance must process vast amounts of data with low latency. Scalability is achieved through high-performance computing clusters, in-memory databases, and optimized C++ code.

Conclusion

In this chapter, we explored the fundamental principles of software architecture that influence scalability, performance, and maintainability. By understanding these core principles, developers can make informed decisions that result in scalable, maintainable, and high-performance applications. As we progress through the following chapters, we will build on this foundation, diving deeper into C++ techniques, patterns, and real-world implementations that help achieve scalable software architecture.

Chapter 2: Modern C++ and Best Practices for Scalable Development

Introduction

This chapter delves into modern C++ features and best practices that play a pivotal role in building scalable software systems. We explore key concepts, language features, and strategies introduced in C++11, C++14, C++17, C++20, and beyond. By adopting these best practices, developers can write code that is not only efficient and maintainable but also scalable to meet the demands of large-scale applications.

1. Embracing Modern C++ Standards

1.1. The Evolution of C++

Modern C++ standards (C++11, C++14, C++17, C++20) have introduced several features that significantly enhance code safety, clarity, and performance. These new standards enable developers to build scalable systems by reducing errors, simplifying syntax, and leveraging more powerful abstractions.

- **Key Improvements in C++11**: Smart pointers, lambda expressions, auto keyword, range-based loops, move semantics.

- **Advancements in C++14 and C++17**: Enhanced lambdas, standardized attributes, parallel algorithms in the STL, optional and variant types.
- **C++20 and Beyond**: Concepts for template constraints, ranges for better collection manipulation, coroutines for asynchronous programming, and enhanced thread support.

Example Expansion: Describe how move semantics introduced in C++11 reduce unnecessary copying of objects, improving performance and scalability.

1.2. Moving Away from Legacy C++

One of the main challenges in scalable development is dealing with legacy codebases that rely on older C++ paradigms and manual memory management. Modern C++ encourages the use of standardized features and idioms to reduce complexity, making the codebase easier to scale and maintain.

- **Replacing Raw Pointers with Smart Pointers**: Using std::shared_ptr, std::unique_ptr, and std::weak_ptr to manage memory safely and effectively.
- **Replacing Manual Loops with Algorithms**: Emphasize using standard algorithms like std::for_each, std::transform, and std::reduce to write concise and readable code.

2. Principles of Modern C++ Development for Scalability

2.1. Resource Management with RAII

Resource Acquisition Is Initialization (RAII) is a core principle in C++ that automatically manages resources like memory, file handles, and network connections. By acquiring resources in constructors and releasing them in destructors, RAII helps prevent resource leaks and improves system stability.

- **Using Smart Pointers for Automatic Memory Management**: Discuss std::unique_ptr for ownership and std::shared_ptr for shared ownership, along with std::make_shared for efficient memory allocation.

2.2. Leveraging Move Semantics and Perfect Forwarding

Move semantics allow developers to transfer ownership of resources instead of duplicating them, which improves performance. Perfect forwarding, enabled by templates, allows functions to forward arguments without unnecessary copying.

- **Example**: Show how move constructors and move assignment operators can reduce the overhead of copying large data structures like vectors or maps.

2.3. Using Type Inference to Enhance Code Readability

Modern C++ provides type inference through the auto and decltype keywords, allowing developers to write concise and clear code. This feature enhances scalability by reducing boilerplate code and focusing on algorithm logic.

2.4. Compile-Time Type Safety with C++ Concepts

Introduced in C++20, concepts provide a way to constrain template parameters, ensuring that only compatible types are used in a generic algorithm or function. This reduces runtime errors and enhances code maintainability.

- **Example**: Show how to use concepts to enforce that a function template only accepts types that support addition and comparison.

3. Concurrency and Parallelism in Modern C++

3.1. Introduction to Concurrency in C++

Concurrency is at the heart of scalable systems, allowing multiple tasks to run simultaneously. Modern C++ offers several features to facilitate concurrent programming, such as the <thread> library, atomic operations, and thread-safe data structures.

- **Using the <thread> Library**: Demonstrate basic thread creation, synchronization with std::mutex and std::condition_variable, and joining or detaching threads.

3.2. Asynchronous Programming with Futures and Promises

Futures and promises provide a mechanism for performing asynchronous tasks without blocking the main thread. They allow developers to write non-blocking code that scales well with large workloads.

- **Example**: Implement an asynchronous data-fetching function using std::async and std::future, showing how to handle exceptions and results.

3.3. Parallel Algorithms in the STL

C++17 introduced parallel versions of standard algorithms (std::for_each, std::sort, etc.), enabling developers to parallelize loops and computations with minimal code changes. Parallel algorithms are crucial for scaling up compute-intensive tasks.

- **Example**: Show how a parallel sort can improve the performance of sorting large data sets by leveraging multiple threads.

4. Design Patterns in Modern C++ for Scalability

4.1. Dependency Injection for Decoupling Components

Dependency Injection (DI) is a design pattern that helps reduce tight coupling between components. By using DI in C++, developers can improve testability and flexibility, making the system easier to scale.

- **Example**: Implement a service registry in C++ that allows components to request and receive dependencies at runtime.

4.2. The Observer Pattern for Event-Driven Systems

The Observer Pattern allows components to subscribe to events and react when the event occurs. This pattern is widely used in scalable, event-driven systems, especially in architectures like microservices.

- **Example**: Show how to use the Observer Pattern to build a notification system that scales with multiple listeners and event types.

4.3. The Factory Pattern for Scalability and Maintainability

The Factory Pattern provides a way to create objects without specifying their concrete classes. This is useful in large-scale systems that require flexibility and ease of maintenance.

- **Example**: Implement a factory class to create different types of network connections based on configuration.

5. Best Practices for Writing Clean and Scalable C++ Code

5.1. Avoiding Memory Leaks and Undefined Behavior

Memory management is one of the most critical aspects of writing scalable C++ applications. Developers must adopt best practices to avoid memory leaks, double deletions, and undefined behavior.

- **Best Practices**:
- Always prefer smart pointers over raw pointers.
- Use memory sanitizers and analyzers to detect leaks and undefined behavior.

5.2. Embracing the DRY (Don't Repeat Yourself) Principle

Repeating code leads to bugs, poor maintainability, and difficulty scaling. The DRY principle helps keep code concise and modular.

- **Example**: Refactor duplicated code into reusable functions or classes to illustrate the impact of the DRY principle on scalability.

5.3. Using Standard Libraries and Avoiding Reinventing the Wheel

C++ offers a wide range of standard libraries for handling common tasks. By leveraging the STL and third-party libraries like Boost, developers can avoid redundant code and focus on higher-level architecture.

- **Example**: Use std::unordered_map for a fast lookup table instead of implementing a custom hash table.

5.4. Profiling and Optimizing Code for Scalability

No matter how well-written the code, performance bottlenecks are inevitable in large-scale systems. Profiling tools like Valgrind, GDB, and Intel VTune can help identify and eliminate these bottlenecks.

- **Steps to Optimize**:
- Identify the most time-consuming functions.
- Optimize data structures and algorithms.
- Use parallelism where appropriate.

6. Real-World Case Studies: Applying Modern C++ for Scalable Systems

6.1. Case Study 1: Building a High-Performance Trading System

This case study examines how a C++ development team designed a scalable, low-latency trading platform capable of processing millions of transactions per second. Key challenges included handling concurrency, managing data integrity, and optimizing performance.

- **Lessons Learned**: Use of low-latency data structures, asynchronous messaging, and efficient memory management.

6.2. Case Study 2: Developing a Scalable Game Engine

Here, we explore how C++ was used to build a modern, scalable game engine that handles real-time physics, rendering, and networking. The focus is on leveraging C++'s power and flexibility to manage complex data structures and computations efficiently.

- **Key Takeaways**: Effective use of multi-threading, parallel algorithms, and design patterns like Entity-Component-System (ECS).

6.3. Case Study 3: Scaling a Cloud-Based Video Streaming Service

This case study covers the architectural decisions involved in scaling a video streaming platform built with C++. The platform had to handle millions of concurrent users, adaptive bitrate streaming, and real-time data analysis.

- **Insights Gained**: Importance of stateless services, efficient use of caching, and distributed data storage.

Conclusion

In this chapter, we explored how modern C++ features and best practices can significantly impact the scalability, performance, and maintainability of software systems. By adopting the principles and techniques discussed, developers can write clean, efficient, and scalable C++ code suitable for large-scale applications. The case studies provided practical insights into the application of these techniques in real-world scenarios.

Chapter 3: Design Patterns and Architectural Paradigms in C++ for Scalable Development

Introduction

D esign patterns and architectural paradigms serve as tried-and-tested solutions to common problems in software design. They are crucial for developers aiming to build scalable systems with C++. This chapter explores essential design patterns and architectural paradigms with practical examples, showing how to effectively leverage them in C++ to achieve scalability, flexibility, and maintainability.

1. The Importance of Design Patterns in Scalable C++ Development

1.1. Defining Design Patterns

Design patterns provide reusable solutions to common problems encountered in software development. They are not specific implementations but rather high-level blueprints for solving problems efficiently and consistently. For scalable software, using patterns like Singleton, Factory, Observer, and more is key to addressing issues like dependency management, object creation, and modularity.

1.2. Benefits of Using Design Patterns

- **Modularity and Decoupling**: Reduces dependencies between different parts of the system, improving maintainability and flexibility.
- **Reusability**: Encourages the reuse of proven solutions, saving development time and reducing errors.
- **Ease of Understanding**: Establishes a common vocabulary for the development team, enhancing communication and understanding.

2. Essential Creational Patterns for Scalable Development

2.1. The Singleton Pattern

The Singleton Pattern ensures a class has only one instance while providing a global point of access to it. This pattern is useful for managing shared resources like logging, configuration, or connection pools.

- **Example**: Implement a thread-safe singleton in C++ using std::mutex to manage a database connection pool.
- **Use Case in Scalability**: Limits resource creation, reducing overhead and simplifying access to shared objects.

2.2. The Factory Method Pattern

The Factory Method Pattern defines an interface for creating objects while allowing subclasses to alter the type of objects created. This pattern helps manage object creation dynamically based on varying runtime conditions.

- **Example**: Implement a factory that creates different types of network sockets (TCP, UDP) based on configuration parameters.
- **Scalability Advantage**: Reduces tight coupling between object creation and application logic, enhancing extensibility.

2.3. The Abstract Factory Pattern

The Abstract Factory Pattern provides an interface for creating families of related objects without specifying their concrete classes. This pattern is useful when your system needs to switch between multiple families of products.

- **Example**: Create an abstract factory for GUI widgets that adapts between different operating systems.
- **Scalability Advantage**: Supports product families, enabling system flexibility as different implementations can be swapped easily.

3. Structural Patterns in Scalable C++ Architecture

3.1. The Adapter Pattern

The Adapter Pattern allows incompatible interfaces to work together by creating a wrapper class that converts the interface of one class into another expected by a client.

- **Example**: Use an adapter to integrate a legacy data storage system with a new RESTful interface.
- **Scalability Benefit**: Facilitates integration of different systems without modifying existing code, improving maintainability.

3.2. The Facade Pattern

The Facade Pattern provides a simplified interface to a complex subsystem. It's especially useful in large-scale systems with multiple interrelated classes and modules.

- **Example**: Create a facade for a video processing system that consolidates functions like encoding, decoding, and streaming.
- **Scalability Benefit**: Simplifies interactions, reducing the learning curve and making the system easier to extend and maintain.

3.3. The Proxy Pattern

The Proxy Pattern provides a surrogate or placeholder for another object to control access to it. It's widely used in distributed systems to manage network calls, resource access, or even for lazy initialization.

- **Example**: Implement a proxy for remote method invocation in a distributed C++ application.
- **Scalability Benefit**: Manages resource-intensive operations efficiently, reducing load and improving response times.

4. Behavioral Patterns for Flexibility and Scalability

4.1. The Observer Pattern

The Observer Pattern establishes a one-to-many relationship between objects, where changes in one object automatically update all dependent objects. This pattern is essential in event-driven and scalable systems.

- **Example**: Implement a notification system for stock market alerts using the Observer Pattern.
- **Scalability Impact**: Decouples event handling from core logic, making it easier to extend and modify event-driven components.

4.2. The Strategy Pattern

The Strategy Pattern defines a family of algorithms, encapsulates each one, and makes them interchangeable. The pattern allows algorithms to vary independently from the clients that use them.

- **Example**: Implement a payment processing system that supports multiple payment strategies (credit card, PayPal, cryptocurrency).
- **Scalability Benefit**: Simplifies adding new strategies without modifying existing code, improving flexibility.

4.3. The Command Pattern

The Command Pattern encapsulates a request as an object, allowing parameterization of clients with queues, logs, and undoable operations. This pattern is useful in applications with a series of operations that need to be executed in different contexts.

- **Example**: Implement a command system for an undo/redo feature in a document editing application.
- **Scalability Benefit**: Enhances command handling capabilities and reduces coupling between invoker and receiver.

5. Architectural Paradigms for Large-Scale C++ Systems

5.1. The Layered Architecture

The Layered Architecture organizes a system into multiple layers, each with a specific responsibility. Common layers include the presentation layer, business logic layer, data access layer, and infrastructure layer.

- **Example**: Design a layered architecture for a RESTful C++ application, where each layer handles specific concerns.
- **Scalability Benefits**: Separates concerns and improves maintainability, allowing individual layers to scale independently.

5.2. The Microservices Architecture

Microservices Architecture involves decomposing an application into smaller, loosely coupled services that communicate over a network. Each service is responsible for a single business capability.

- **Example**: Design a microservices architecture for an e-commerce platform, with separate services for inventory management, user authentication, and payment processing.
- **Scalability Advantage**: Enables independent scaling of each service based on demand, improving system resilience and flexibility.

5.3. The Event-Driven Architecture (EDA)

Event-Driven Architecture focuses on asynchronous communication between services through events. It's ideal for systems that require high responsiveness and real-time processing.

- **Example**: Implement an event-driven system for a messaging application that handles user messages, notifications, and chat rooms.
- **Scalability Benefits**: Decouples components and improves real-time responsiveness, allowing the system to scale seamlessly with increased load.

5.4. The Domain-Driven Design (DDD) Approach

Domain-Driven Design emphasizes creating a model based on the business domain and its logic. DDD uses concepts like bounded contexts, aggregates, and domain events to align software architecture with business requirements.

- **Example**: Apply DDD to a banking application with bounded contexts like customer accounts, transactions, and loans.
- **Scalability Benefit**: Promotes a clear separation of domains, enabling independent evolution and scaling of each bounded context.

6. Real-World Case Studies: Applying Design Patterns and Architectures

6.1. Case Study 1: Scalable Cloud-Based E-Commerce Platform

Explore how a C++ development team used a combination of microservices and event-driven architecture to build a cloud-based e-commerce platform. The case study includes the use of design patterns like the Observer and Strategy patterns to achieve modularity and flexibility.

6.2. Case Study 2: Real-Time Financial Trading System

Analyze how a real-time trading platform leveraged C++ for low-latency processing, using layered architecture and behavioral patterns like Command and Strategy to manage trading algorithms and market data efficiently.

6.3. Case Study 3: High-Performance Game Engine

Study the design of a high-performance game engine with a focus on using the Entity-Component-System (ECS) architecture for game objects. Explore how the Observer Pattern and Facade Pattern were used to manage game events and subsystem interactions.

Conclusion

In this chapter, we explored essential design patterns and architectural paradigms for building scalable software systems in C++. Each design pattern and architectural paradigm contributes to enhancing modularity, flexibility, and maintainability. By understanding and applying these patterns, developers can build scalable systems that efficiently handle increasing workloads and evolving requirements. Real-world case studies provided practical insights into the implementation of these techniques.

Chapter 4: Concurrency and Parallelism in C++

Introduction

oncurrency and parallelism are essential for building scalable and efficient software systems. With the increasing need for real-time processing and high-performance computing, mastering concurrency and parallelism in C++ is crucial. This chapter delves into the foundational concepts, key techniques, and practical examples to help you write scalable and concurrent C++ applications.

1. Fundamentals of Concurrency and Parallelism

1.1. Understanding Concurrency and Parallelism

Concurrency refers to the execution of multiple tasks or processes simultaneously within a system. Parallelism, on the other hand, focuses on performing multiple operations at the same time by utilizing multiple processors or cores. While the two concepts are closely related, concurrency is more about task management, while parallelism emphasizes simultaneous execution.

- **Concurrency in C++**: Managing multiple threads and coordinating their tasks effectively.
- **Parallelism in C++**: Maximizing CPU core utilization through parallel execution of independent operations.

1.2. The Importance of Concurrency and Parallelism

In today's multi-core processor environment, efficient software must leverage concurrency and parallelism to handle large volumes of data, multiple users, and real-time processing requirements. High-performance systems like financial trading platforms, gaming engines, and large-scale web servers depend on these principles to achieve scalability and responsiveness.

1.3. Concurrency vs. Parallelism: Key Differences

Concurrency involves the execution of multiple tasks in an overlapping manner, where tasks share resources and execute concurrently. Parallelism involves splitting a task into sub-tasks that are executed simultaneously on different cores. Understanding these differences is critical when designing and implementing scalable systems.

2. C++ Concurrency Tools and Techniques

2.1. The <thread> Library

The C++ <thread> library provides an essential foundation for creating and managing threads. Introduced in C++11, it simplifies multi-threaded programming by abstracting thread creation, management, and synchronization.

- **Creating and Managing Threads**: Explain how to create threads using std::thread and manage their lifecycles using join and detach operations.
- **Example**: Write a simple program that creates multiple threads to perform different tasks, such as reading files or processing data.

2.2. Mutexes and Locking Mechanisms

Concurrency often leads to issues like data races and deadlocks, which occur when multiple threads try to access shared resources simultaneously. C++ provides mutexes (std::mutex) to prevent data races and ensure that only one thread accesses a shared resource at a time.

- **Using Mutexes to Avoid Data Races**: Describe how to use std::mutex and std::lock_guard to protect critical sections.
- **Avoiding Deadlocks with Scoped Locks**: Discuss std::unique_lock and std::scoped_lock to prevent deadlocks by managing multiple mutexes.

2.3. Condition Variables for Synchronization

Condition variables (std::condition_variable) allow threads to wait for certain conditions to be met before proceeding. They are essential for coordinating thread execution and synchronizing tasks that rely on shared resources.

- **Example**: Demonstrate how to use condition variables to synchronize a producer-consumer problem in C++.

2.4. Atomic Operations for Lock-Free Programming

C++ provides atomic types (std::atomic) to perform thread-safe operations without using locks. Lock-free programming is crucial in scenarios requiring high concurrency, such as real-time systems.

- **Using std::atomic for Performance Optimization**: Explain how to use atomic variables to implement efficient counters or flags in a multi-threaded application.
- **Example**: Implement a lock-free queue using atomic pointers and explain the advantages of lock-free programming.

3. Advanced Concurrency Features in Modern C++

3.1. Using std::async for Asynchronous Tasks

std::async provides a higher-level abstraction for launching asynchronous tasks. It allows you to run functions asynchronously and retrieve their results using std::future.

- **Example**: Write a program that performs multiple file I/O operations asynchronously using std::async and demonstrates how to manage task results with std::future.

3.2. Promises and Futures for Asynchronous Communication

Promises and futures provide a mechanism for communication between threads. A promise is used to set a value or an exception, while a future is used to retrieve that value.

- **Example**: Implement a simple chat server using promises and futures for asynchronous message passing.

3.3. Thread Pools for Efficient Resource Management

A thread pool is a collection of pre-initialized threads ready to perform tasks. Thread pools are ideal for managing a large number of short-lived tasks efficiently, reducing the overhead of creating and destroying threads repeatedly.

- **Creating a Thread Pool**: Explain the basics of a thread pool implementation in C++, focusing on task queues and worker threads.
- **Example**: Implement a simple thread pool that schedules and executes multiple tasks concurrently.

3.4. Parallel Algorithms in C++17 and Beyond

C++17 introduced parallel algorithms in the Standard Template Library (STL), allowing developers to leverage parallelism without manually managing threads. Algorithms like std::for_each, std::sort, and std::reduce can now be executed in parallel using policies like std::execution::par.

- **Example**: Show how to use parallel algorithms to perform large-scale data processing, demonstrating performance improvements with parallel execution.

4. Common Pitfalls in Concurrency and How to Avoid Them

4.1. Data Races and How to Prevent Them

Data races occur when two or more threads access shared data simultaneously without proper synchronization. They can lead to unpredictable behavior, crashes, and data corruption.

- **Using Mutexes and Atomic Variables**: Explain how to use mutexes and atomic variables to prevent data races effectively.

4.2. Deadlocks and Techniques for Deadlock Avoidance

Deadlocks occur when two or more threads are waiting for each other to release resources, resulting in a system freeze. Deadlock prevention requires careful resource management and locking strategies.

- **Techniques for Deadlock Avoidance**: Discuss common techniques such as ordered locking, avoiding circular dependencies, and using timed locks.

4.3. Starvation and Priority Inversion

Starvation occurs when lower-priority threads are perpetually delayed due to higher-priority threads occupying resources. Priority inversion happens when lower-priority tasks block higher-priority tasks due to shared resources.

- **Solutions to Starvation and Priority Inversion**: Explore techniques like priority boosting, avoiding long locks, and implementing fair scheduling policies.

5. Practical Applications of Concurrency and Parallelism in C++

5.1. Real-Time Data Processing in Financial Systems

Financial systems like stock trading platforms require real-time processing of market data. These systems must handle large volumes of data with low latency to ensure timely and accurate decision-making.

- **Concurrency in Trading Algorithms**: Discuss how to implement multi-threaded trading algorithms that analyze market trends and execute trades simultaneously.

5.2. Concurrent Networking in C++

Networking applications, such as chat servers or multiplayer games, must handle multiple client connections simultaneously. Concurrency allows these applications to manage I/O operations and communication efficiently.

- **Example**: Implement a multi-threaded chat server that handles multiple clients using asynchronous I/O and threads.

5.3. Multi-Threaded Game Engines

Modern game engines rely heavily on concurrency and parallelism to handle physics simulations, AI, rendering, and input processing. Efficient multi-threading is crucial to delivering a smooth gaming experience.

- **Concurrency in Game Loops**: Discuss techniques for dividing game loops into multiple concurrent tasks, such as physics updates, rendering, and input handling.

6. Case Studies: Real-World Applications of Concurrency and Parallelism

6.1. Case Study 1: High-Performance Trading Platform

Explore how a trading platform used C++ concurrency features like asynchronous I/O, atomic operations, and parallel algorithms to achieve low-latency, high-frequency trading capabilities.

- **Challenges Faced and Solutions Implemented**: Discuss the challenges of data races, synchronization, and latency in a high-stakes trading environment and the architectural solutions adopted.

6.2. Case Study 2: Concurrent Video Processing System

Analyze the development of a concurrent video processing system built with C++. The system handles tasks like video encoding, streaming, and filtering using thread pools and parallel algorithms.

- **Scalability and Performance Improvements**: Highlight the performance gains achieved through parallelism and efficient resource management.

6.3. Case Study 3: Multi-Threaded Web Server

Examine how a multi-threaded web server in C++ was designed to handle large numbers of simultaneous client requests. Discuss the use of thread pools, I/O multiplexing, and synchronization techniques.

- **Balancing Throughput and Latency**: Discuss the trade-offs involved in balancing throughput and latency in a concurrent server architecture.

Conclusion

Concurrency and parallelism are indispensable tools for building scalable and high-performance C++ applications. By leveraging modern C++ features like threads, mutexes, atomics, and parallel algorithms, developers can design systems that efficiently utilize multi-core processors and handle increasing workloads. In this chapter, we explored the fundamental concepts, advanced techniques, and real-world applications of concurrency and parallel

Chapter 5: Best Practices for Writing Clean and Scalable C++ Code

Introduction

I n this chapter, we will explore the best practices for writing clean and scalable C++ code. Clean code is easier to read, maintain, and extend, while scalable code efficiently manages resources and handles increasing loads. We will cover topics such as coding standards, effective use of modern C++ features, memory management, error handling, testing, and optimization techniques. Adopting these practices will ensure your codebase is robust, maintainable, and ready for scaling as demands grow.

1. Coding Standards and Guidelines

1.1. Importance of Coding Standards

Coding standards provide a consistent style and structure for your code, making it easier for teams to collaborate and understand each other's work. They help in reducing bugs, improving readability, and ensuring maintainability.

- **Key Benefits:**

- **Consistency**: Uniformity in code style enhances readability and comprehension.
- **Collaboration**: Standardized code allows team members to easily understand and modify each other's work.
- **Reduced Bugs**: Following established patterns can prevent common pitfalls and errors.

1.2. Common Coding Standards in C++

Many organizations adopt specific coding standards. A few well-known ones include:

- **Google C++ Style Guide**: Emphasizes readability, clear naming conventions, and proper structuring.
- **C++ Core Guidelines**: Provides guidelines for safe and efficient C++ coding, emphasizing the use of modern features and best practices.

Example Expansion: Detail specific rules, such as naming conventions (e.g., CamelCase for classes, snake_case for variables), indentation styles, and comment usage.

1.3. Code Reviews and Pair Programming

Conducting regular code reviews and using pair programming can significantly improve code quality. Code reviews help identify issues early, while pair programming fosters knowledge sharing and adherence to standards.

- **Benefits of Code Reviews**:
- Early detection of bugs and inconsistencies.
- Knowledge transfer between team members.
- Enhanced team cohesion and collaboration.

2. Leveraging Modern C++ Features

2.1. Smart Pointers for Memory Management

Modern C++ provides smart pointers (std::unique_ptr, std::shared_ptr, std::weak_ptr) that automatically manage memory, reducing the risk of memory leaks and dangling pointers.

- **Using std::unique_ptr**: For exclusive ownership, ensuring that an object is deleted when it goes out of scope.
- **Using std::shared_ptr**: For shared ownership, allowing multiple pointers to own the same resource without manual memory management.

Example Expansion: Illustrate the use of smart pointers in a simple application, showing the differences between raw pointers and smart pointers in terms of memory management.

2.2. Range-Based For Loops

Range-based for loops, introduced in C++11, provide a more readable and less error-prone way to iterate over containers.

- **Example**: Compare traditional for loops with range-based for loops, emphasizing clarity and conciseness.

2.3. Lambda Expressions for Inline Functions

Lambdas allow developers to define anonymous functions inline, enhancing readability and flexibility when passing functions as parameters.

- **Example**: Use lambdas for sorting and filtering collections, demonstrating their utility in modern C++ programming.

3. Effective Memory Management Techniques

3.1. Understanding Memory Allocation
Efficient memory management is critical for scalable applications. Understanding stack vs. heap allocation and the costs associated with each can lead to better performance.

- **Stack vs. Heap**: Discuss the differences in allocation speed, lifetime, and management between stack and heap memory.

3.2. Avoiding Memory Leaks
Memory leaks occur when dynamically allocated memory is not released. To prevent memory leaks:

- **Use Smart Pointers**: Always prefer smart pointers to manage dynamic memory automatically.
- **Regularly Analyze Code**: Use tools like Valgrind to check for memory leaks and address them promptly.

3.3. Pool Allocators for Performance
Pool allocators manage memory in fixed-size blocks, improving performance in systems that allocate and deallocate memory frequently.

- **Example**: Implement a simple pool allocator and demonstrate its efficiency in managing memory for a large number of small objects.

4. Error Handling and Exception Safety

4.1. The Importance of Error Handling
Robust error handling is essential for building reliable applications. C++ provides exceptions for handling errors gracefully.

4.2. Using Exceptions Effectively
When using exceptions, it's crucial to adhere to best practices to maintain

program stability.

- **Throwing Exceptions**: Use exceptions for unexpected conditions and avoid using them for control flow.
- **Catching Exceptions**: Catch exceptions by reference to avoid unnecessary copies.

4.3. Exception Safety Levels

C++ provides three levels of exception safety: no guarantee, strong guarantee, and basic guarantee. Understand these levels to write robust code.

- **Example**: Discuss strategies to achieve strong exception safety, such as using the copy-and-swap idiom.

5. Writing Tests and Ensuring Code Quality

5.1. Importance of Testing in C++ Development

Testing is a critical aspect of software development that ensures code quality and functionality. Unit tests, integration tests, and system tests help catch bugs early and improve code reliability.

5.2. Unit Testing with Google Test

Google Test is a popular framework for writing unit tests in C++. It provides a rich set of assertions and test fixtures.

- **Example**: Write a simple unit test using Google Test to demonstrate how to set up a test case and check for expected outcomes.

5.3. Test-Driven Development (TDD)

Test-Driven Development emphasizes writing tests before the code itself. This practice helps clarify requirements and improve design.

- **Example**: Show how to implement a simple function using TDD principles, iterating through writing tests, coding, and refactoring.

6. Performance Optimization Techniques

6.1. Profiling and Benchmarking
Before optimizing, it's crucial to profile the code to identify bottlenecks. Profiling tools help pinpoint which parts of the code are slow or resource-intensive.

- **Popular Profiling Tools**: Discuss tools like gprof, Valgrind, and Intel VTune for profiling C++ applications.

6.2. Common Optimization Techniques

- **Inlining Functions**: Reduce function call overhead by using inline functions for small, frequently called functions.
- **Reducing Object Creation**: Minimize dynamic memory allocations in performance-critical sections.

Example Expansion: Provide a case study that illustrates the impact of optimization techniques on application performance.

6.3. Compiler Optimizations
Leverage compiler optimizations to enhance performance without changing the code.

- **Using Compiler Flags**: Discuss how to use optimization flags (e.g., -O2, -O3) to improve performance during the build process.

7. Documentation and Code Comments

7.1. The Importance of Documentation
Good documentation helps maintain clarity and usability in the codebase. It's essential for new developers joining the project and for long-term

maintenance.

7.2. Writing Effective Code Comments

While comments are crucial, over-commenting can lead to clutter. Aim for clarity and conciseness.

- **When to Comment**: Document the "why" behind complex algorithms rather than stating the obvious.
- **Example**: Compare well-documented code with poorly documented code to illustrate best practices.

8. Real-World Case Studies: Best Practices in Action

8.1. Case Study 1: High-Performance Data Processing Application

Explore how a data processing application implemented best practices for clean and scalable C++ code. Discuss the benefits gained from effective memory management, testing, and profiling.

8.2. Case Study 2: Multi-Threaded Game Development

Analyze a multi-threaded game development project that adhered to modern C++ standards and best practices, leading to improved performance and maintainability.

8.3. Case Study 3: Scalable Web Server Implementation

Examine how a scalable web server was developed using C++ best practices, focusing on concurrency, error handling, and testing methodologies.

Conclusion

In this chapter, we covered best practices for writing clean and scalable C++ code. From coding standards and memory management techniques to effective error handling and performance optimization, these practices are essential for developing robust and maintainable applications. By adopting these strategies, developers can ensure that their code is not only functional but also scalable, ready to meet the demands of growing systems. As we move forward, we will continue to explore advanced topics in software architecture and design patterns to further enhance your skills in scalable C++ development.

Chapter 6: Advanced C++ Techniques for Scalable Software Development

Introduction

In the realm of scalable software development, mastering advanced techniques in C++ is essential for building robust and efficient applications. This chapter delves into sophisticated programming concepts and tools that enhance scalability, performance, and maintainability in C++. We will explore template metaprogramming, advanced memory management, custom data structures, and performance optimization strategies that leverage the full power of modern C++. By understanding and applying these techniques, developers can create applications that not only perform well but are also adaptable to changing requirements and increased loads.

1. Template Metaprogramming

1.1. Understanding Templates in C++

Templates are a powerful feature of C++ that allows developers to write generic and reusable code. They enable the creation of functions and classes that work with any data type without sacrificing type safety. There are two main types of templates: function templates and class templates.

- **Function Templates**: Allow you to define a function that can operate with any data type.
- **Example**:

```cpp
Copy code
template<typename T>
T add(T a, T b) {
    return a + b;
}
```

- **Class Templates**: Enable the creation of classes that can handle different data types.
- **Example**:

```cpp
Copy code
template<typename T>
class Container {
    T element;
public:
    Container(T elem) : element(elem) {}
    T getElement() const { return element; }
};
```

1.2. Benefits of Template Metaprogramming

Template metaprogramming takes advantage of C++ templates to perform computations at compile time rather than runtime. This can lead to significant performance improvements.

- **Compile-Time Computation**: Use templates to calculate values during

45

compilation, reducing runtime overhead.

- **Example**:

```cpp
Copy code
template<int N>
struct Factorial {
    static const int value = N * Factorial<N - 1>::value;
};
template<>
struct Factorial<0> {
    static const int value = 1;
};
```

- **Type Traits and SFINAE**: Use type traits and the SFINAE (Substitution Failure Is Not An Error) principle to create more flexible and type-safe generic code.

1.3. SFINAE and Type Traits

SFINAE allows you to enable or disable function templates based on type properties, providing a way to implement more sophisticated template logic.

- **Type Traits**: Use type traits to determine properties of types at compile time.
- **Example**:

```cpp
Copy code
template<typename T>
typename std::enable_if<std::is_integral<T>::value, T>::type
increment(T value) {
    return value + 1;
```

```
}
```

- **Function Overloading with SFINAE**: Demonstrate how SFINAE can be used to provide different implementations based on the type of arguments passed.

2. Advanced Memory Management Techniques

2.1. Custom Allocators

While smart pointers simplify memory management, custom allocators can optimize memory allocation for specific use cases, improving performance and reducing fragmentation.

- **Creating a Custom Allocator**: Define a custom allocator that manages memory for a specific data structure or application.
- **Example**:

```cpp
Copy code
template<typename T>
struct PoolAllocator {
    using value_type = T;

    PoolAllocator() = default;

    template<typename U>
    PoolAllocator(const PoolAllocator<U>&) {}

    T* allocate(std::size_t n) {
        return static_cast<T*>(::operator new(n * sizeof(T)));
    }

    void deallocate(T* p, std::size_t) {
```

```
            ::operator delete(p);
    }
};
```

2.2. Resource Management Strategies

Effective resource management involves understanding the lifetimes of objects and ensuring they are properly cleaned up to prevent leaks.

- **RAII (Resource Acquisition Is Initialization)**: Use RAII principles to manage resources, ensuring that resources are acquired and released properly.
- **Scope-Based Resource Management**: Discuss techniques for managing resource lifetimes using scope-based strategies, ensuring resources are cleaned up when they go out of scope.

3. Designing Custom Data Structures

3.1. The Importance of Custom Data Structures

In many cases, standard data structures may not meet the performance requirements of specific applications. Custom data structures can be designed to optimize performance for specific scenarios.

- **When to Use Custom Structures**: Analyze the scenarios where using standard libraries may lead to performance bottlenecks.

3.2. Implementing a Custom Linked List

Building a custom linked list can illustrate the advantages of tailored data structures.

- **Custom Linked List Implementation**:

```cpp
Copy code
template<typename T>
class LinkedList {
    struct Node {
        T data;
        Node* next;
        Node(T val) : data(val), next(nullptr) {}
    };
    Node* head;
public:
    LinkedList() : head(nullptr) {}
    void push_back(T val) {
        Node* newNode = new Node(val);
        if (!head) {
            head = newNode;
        } else {
            Node* temp = head;
            while (temp->next) temp = temp->next;
            temp->next = newNode;
        }
    }
    // Other methods...
};
```

3.3. Performance Considerations

Discuss the performance trade-offs of using custom data structures compared to standard containers, including memory overhead, allocation speed, and cache locality.

4. Optimizing Performance in C++ Applications

4.1. Profiling and Identifying Bottlenecks

Before optimizing code, it is critical to profile it to identify performance bottlenecks. Profiling tools help determine which parts of the code are slow or resource-intensive.

- **Using Profiling Tools**: Introduce tools like Valgrind, gprof, and Intel VTune for profiling applications.

4.2. Common Optimization Techniques

- **Loop Unrolling**: Optimize loops to reduce overhead by manually unrolling them, improving performance in compute-intensive scenarios.
- **Inlining Functions**: Use the inline keyword to reduce function call overhead for small functions that are called frequently.
- **Reducing Object Creation**: Minimize dynamic memory allocations by reusing objects or using stack allocation when possible.

4.3. Compiler Optimizations

Leverage compiler optimizations to improve performance without altering the code.

- **Optimization Flags**: Explain how to use flags like -O2 and -O3 for GCC or Clang to enable various optimization levels during compilation.

5. Error Handling and Exception Safety

5.1. Effective Use of Exceptions

Exceptions provide a robust way to handle errors in C++. Properly using exceptions can prevent crashes and improve code reliability.

- **Best Practices for Exceptions**:
- Always catch exceptions by reference.
- Use specific exception types to provide meaningful error handling.

5.2. Exception Safety Levels

C++ applications should adhere to levels of exception safety, ensuring that functions guarantee specific behavior in the presence of exceptions.

- **Strong Guarantee**: Ensure that operations are either completed successfully or have no side effects.
- **Basic Guarantee**: Ensure that the program remains in a valid state, even if an exception is thrown.

Example Expansion: Provide code examples that illustrate how to achieve strong exception safety using the copy-and-swap idiom.

6. Unit Testing and Test-Driven Development (TDD)

6.1. The Importance of Unit Testing

Unit testing is vital for ensuring the correctness of individual components in C++ applications. It helps catch bugs early and improves overall software quality.

6.2. Using Google Test for Unit Testing

Google Test is a widely used framework for writing unit tests in C++. It provides a rich set of assertions and testing utilities.

- **Writing Test Cases**: Demonstrate how to set up and write basic test cases using Google Test.
- **Example**:

```cpp
Copy code
#include <gtest/gtest.h>

TEST(MyTestSuite, Addition) {
    EXPECT_EQ(add(2, 3), 5);
}
```

6.3. Test-Driven Development (TDD)

Test-Driven Development emphasizes writing tests before the code itself. This approach clarifies requirements and leads to better-designed software.

- **TDD Cycle**: Discuss the TDD cycle: Red (failing tests), Green (passing tests), Refactor (improve the code).

7. Code Review and Refactoring

7.1. The Role of Code Reviews
Code reviews are an essential practice for maintaining code quality. They help catch errors, enforce coding standards, and facilitate knowledge sharing among team members.

- **Best Practices for Code Reviews**: Establish clear guidelines for conducting effective code reviews.

7.2. Refactoring for Maintainability
Refactoring is the process of restructuring existing code without changing its external behavior. It improves code readability and maintainability.

- **When to Refactor**: Identify signs that code needs refactoring, such as code smells, duplications, or overly complex logic.

8. Real-World Applications of Advanced Techniques

8.1. Case Study 1: High-Performance Game Engine
Explore how a game engine utilizes advanced C++ techniques for memory management, concurrency, and performance optimization to deliver a high-quality gaming experience.

8.2. Case Study 2: Real-Time Financial Analytics Platform
Analyze a financial analytics platform built with C++, focusing on template metaprogramming, custom data structures, and performance profiling to handle vast amounts of data efficiently.

8.3. Case Study 3: Scalable Cloud-Based Web Application
Examine how a cloud-based web application leverages modern C++ features and best practices to ensure scalability, maintainability, and per-

formance.

Conclusion

In this chapter, we explored advanced C++ techniques for scalable software development. By leveraging template metaprogramming, custom data structures, and performance optimization strategies, developers can create efficient and maintainable applications. Implementing best practices for memory management, error handling, testing, and code review ensures that the software remains robust and adaptable to changing demands. As we continue to delve into more advanced topics, we will see how these techniques can be combined with architectural patterns to build truly scalable systems.

Chapter 7: Design Patterns in C++ for Scalable Software Development

Introduction

D esign patterns are essential building blocks for scalable software development. They provide time-tested solutions to common design problems, allowing developers to create flexible, reusable, and maintainable code. This chapter explores various design patterns applicable in C++, focusing on their implementation and how they contribute to scalable architecture. We will discuss creational, structural, and behavioral patterns, providing examples and insights into their practical applications.

1. Creational Patterns

Creational patterns deal with object creation mechanisms, aiming to create objects in a manner suitable to the situation. They abstract the instantiation process, making the system independent of how its objects are created, composed, and represented.

1.1. Singleton Pattern

The Singleton Pattern ensures a class has only one instance and provides a global point of access to that instance. This pattern is particularly useful when exactly one object is needed to coordinate actions across the system.

- **Implementation**: In C++, the Singleton Pattern can be implemented using a private constructor and a static method that returns the instance of the class.

Example:

```cpp
Copy code
class Singleton {
private:
    static Singleton* instance;

    // Private constructor
    Singleton() {}

public:
    // Static method to control access to the instance
    static Singleton* getInstance() {
        if (!instance) {
            instance = new Singleton();
        }
        return instance;
    }
};

// Initialize static member
Singleton* Singleton::instance = nullptr;
```

- **Scalability Considerations**: The Singleton Pattern can help manage shared resources, such as configuration settings or logging services, ensuring that multiple parts of the application can access these resources consistently.

1.2. Factory Method Pattern

The Factory Method Pattern defines an interface for creating objects but allows subclasses to alter the type of created objects. This pattern promotes loose coupling by removing the dependency on concrete classes.

- **Implementation**: The Factory Method involves creating an interface for the object creation and implementing that interface in subclasses.

Example:

```cpp
Copy code
class Product {
public:
    virtual void use() = 0; // Pure virtual function
};

class ConcreteProductA : public Product {
public:
    void use() override {
        std::cout << "Using Product A" << std::endl;
    }
};

class ConcreteProductB : public Product {
public:
    void use() override {
        std::cout << "Using Product B" << std::endl;
    }
};

class Creator {
public:
    virtual Product* factoryMethod() = 0; // Factory method
};

class ConcreteCreatorA : public Creator {
public:
    Product* factoryMethod() override {
```

```cpp
        return new ConcreteProductA();
    }
};

class ConcreteCreatorB : public Creator {
public:
    Product* factoryMethod() override {
        return new ConcreteProductB();
    }
};
```

- **Scalability Considerations**: The Factory Method Pattern allows for easy extension of the system with new product types without modifying existing code, facilitating scalability.

1.3. Abstract Factory Pattern

The Abstract Factory Pattern provides an interface for creating families of related or dependent objects without specifying their concrete classes. This pattern is useful when a system should be independent of how its products are created, composed, and represented.

- **Implementation**: The Abstract Factory defines a set of factory methods for creating related products.

Example:

```cpp
cpp
Copy code
class AbstractProductA {
public:
    virtual void use() = 0;
};
```

```cpp
class AbstractProductB {
public:
    virtual void use() = 0;
};

class ConcreteProductA1 : public AbstractProductA {
public:
    void use() override {
        std::cout << "Using Product A1" << std::endl;
    }
};

class ConcreteProductB1 : public AbstractProductB {
public:
    void use() override {
        std::cout << "Using Product B1" << std::endl;
    }
};

class AbstractFactory {
public:
    virtual AbstractProductA* createProductA() = 0;
    virtual AbstractProductB* createProductB() = 0;
};

class ConcreteFactory1 : public AbstractFactory {
public:
    AbstractProductA* createProductA() override {
        return new ConcreteProductA1();
    }
    AbstractProductB* createProductB() override {
        return new ConcreteProductB1();
    }
};
```

- **Scalability Considerations**: The Abstract Factory Pattern supports the creation of complex systems with multiple product families, allowing for flexible configuration and easy addition of new product families.

2. Structural Patterns

Structural patterns deal with object composition and relationships between objects. They help ensure that if one part of a system changes, the entire system doesn't need to change.

2.1. Adapter Pattern

The Adapter Pattern allows incompatible interfaces to work together. It acts as a bridge between two incompatible interfaces, enabling them to communicate.

- **Implementation**: The Adapter wraps an existing class with a new interface.

Example:

```cpp
Copy code
class Target {
public:
    virtual void request() {
        std::cout << "Target: Default request." << std::endl;
    }
};

class Adaptee {
public:
    void specificRequest() {
        std::cout << "Adaptee: Specific request." << std::endl;
    }
};

class Adapter : public Target {
private:
    Adaptee* adaptee;
public:
    Adapter(Adaptee* a) : adaptee(a) {}
```

```cpp
    void request() override {
        adaptee->specificRequest();
    }
};
```

- **Scalability Considerations**: The Adapter Pattern is useful when integrating legacy systems with new architectures, enabling scalability without the need for extensive changes.

2.2. Facade Pattern

The Facade Pattern provides a simplified interface to a complex subsystem. It defines a higher-level interface that makes the subsystem easier to use.

- **Implementation**: The Facade creates a unified interface for a set of interfaces in a subsystem.

Example:

```cpp
cpp
Copy code
class SubsystemA {
public:
    void operationA() {
        std::cout << "Subsystem A: Operation A" << std::endl;
    }
};

class SubsystemB {
public:
    void operationB() {
        std::cout << "Subsystem B: Operation B" << std::endl;
    }
};
```

```cpp
class Facade {
private:
    SubsystemA* subsystemA;
    SubsystemB* subsystemB;
public:
    Facade() {
        subsystemA = new SubsystemA();
        subsystemB = new SubsystemB();
    }
    void operation() {
        subsystemA->operationA();
        subsystemB->operationB();
    }
};
```

- **Scalability Considerations**: The Facade Pattern simplifies the interactions between complex subsystems, making it easier to extend or modify the system.

2.3. Composite Pattern

The Composite Pattern allows you to compose objects into tree structures to represent part-whole hierarchies. It enables clients to treat individual objects and compositions uniformly.

- **Implementation**: The Composite Pattern consists of leaf nodes and composite nodes.

Example:

```cpp
cpp
Copy code
class Component {
public:
    virtual void operation() = 0;
```

```
};

class Leaf : public Component {
public:
    void operation() override {
        std::cout << "Leaf operation" << std::endl;
    }
};

class Composite : public Component {
private:
    std::vector<Component*> children;
public:
    void add(Component* component) {
        children.push_back(component);
    }
    void operation() override {
        std::cout << "Composite operation" << std::endl;
        for (auto& child : children) {
            child->operation();
        }
    }
};
```

- **Scalability Considerations**: The Composite Pattern is beneficial for building hierarchical structures, such as file systems or UI components, allowing for easy addition of new components.

3. Behavioral Patterns

Behavioral patterns focus on communication between objects, defining how objects interact in a system.

3.1. Observer Pattern

The Observer Pattern establishes a one-to-many relationship between objects, allowing one object (the subject) to notify multiple observers about changes in its state.

- **Implementation**: The Subject maintains a list of observers and notifies them of any state changes.

Example:

```cpp
Copy code
class Observer {
public:
    virtual void update() = 0;
};

class Subject {
private:
    std::vector<Observer*> observers;
public:
    void attach(Observer* observer) {
        observers.push_back(observer);
    }
    void notify() {
        for (auto& observer : observers) {
            observer->update();
        }
    }
};

class ConcreteObserver : public Observer {
public:
    void update() override {
        std::cout << "Observer updated." << std::endl;
    }
};
```

- **Scalability Considerations**: The Observer Pattern allows for loose coupling between components, making it easier to extend the system with new observers.

3.2. Strategy Pattern

The Strategy Pattern defines a family of algorithms, encapsulates each one, and makes them interchangeable. This pattern allows the algorithm to vary independently from the clients that use it.

- **Implementation**: The Strategy Pattern involves a context that uses different strategies at runtime.

Example:

```cpp
Copy code
class Strategy {
public:
    virtual void execute() = 0;
};

class ConcreteStrategyA : public Strategy {
public:
    void execute() override {
        std::cout << "Executing Strategy A" << std::endl;
    }
};

class ConcreteStrategyB : public Strategy {
public:
    void execute() override {
        std::cout << "Executing Strategy B" << std::endl;
    }
};

class Context {
private:
    Strategy* strategy;
public:
    void setStrategy(Strategy* s) {
        strategy = s;
    }
```

```cpp
    void executeStrategy() {
        strategy->execute();
    }
};
```

- **Scalability Considerations**: The Strategy Pattern promotes flexibility and reusability, making it easier to introduce new algorithms without modifying existing code.

3.3. Command Pattern

The Command Pattern encapsulates a request as an object, allowing parameterization of clients with queues, logs, and undoable operations. This pattern separates the object that invokes the operation from the one that knows how to perform it.

- **Implementation**: Commands are created as objects, allowing for operations to be queued, logged, or undone.

Example:

```cpp
cpp
Copy code
class Command {
public:
    virtual void execute() = 0;
};

class ConcreteCommand : public Command {
private:
    Receiver* receiver;
public:
    ConcreteCommand(Receiver* r) : receiver(r) {}
    void execute() override {
        receiver->action();
```

```
    }
};

class Invoker {
private:
    Command* command;
public:
    void setCommand(Command* c) {
        command = c;
    }
    void invoke() {
        command->execute();
    }
};
```

- **Scalability Considerations**: The Command Pattern allows for flexible request handling and supports features like undo functionality, making the system easier to extend.

4. Choosing the Right Design Patterns

4.1. Identifying Patterns Based on Requirements
When building scalable systems, it's essential to choose the right design patterns based on specific requirements. Consider the following factors:

- **System Complexity**: For simple applications, a few well-chosen patterns may suffice. In contrast, complex systems might benefit from multiple patterns working together.
- **Flexibility and Extensibility**: Identify patterns that promote flexibility and allow for easy extensions or modifications in the future.

4.2. Combining Patterns for Enhanced Scalability
Design patterns can often be combined to address more complex requirements. For example, using the Factory Method in conjunction with the

Singleton Pattern can create a single instance of a factory that produces objects.

- **Example**: Discuss how the Strategy Pattern can be combined with the Observer Pattern in a real-time data processing application, allowing for dynamic algorithm selection while notifying interested parties of state changes.

5. Real-World Applications of Design Patterns in C++

5.1. Case Study 1: Building a Scalable E-Commerce Platform
Explore how an e-commerce platform utilizes various design patterns to handle different aspects of the system, including the Observer Pattern for managing notifications, the Strategy Pattern for payment processing, and the Factory Method for product creation.

5.2. Case Study 2: Developing a Multi-Player Online Game
Analyze how design patterns like Command, Observer, and State are employed in a multi-player online game to manage player actions, game state changes, and UI updates effectively.

5.3. Case Study 3: Implementing a Financial Trading System
Examine a financial trading system that leverages the Singleton, Factory Method, and Strategy Patterns to manage trading strategies, execute orders, and maintain a single instance of the trading engine.

Conclusion

In this chapter, we explored various design patterns relevant to scalable software development in C++. From creational patterns that streamline object creation to structural patterns that facilitate object composition, and behavioral patterns that define communication between objects, understanding these patterns is essential for building robust and scalable applications. Through practical examples and real-world case studies, we have demonstrated how to implement these patterns effectively. By applying these design patterns, developers can enhance the flexibility, maintainability, and scalability of their C++ applications, paving the way for future growth and adaptability.

Chapter 8: Testing and Quality Assurance in C++ for Scalable Software Development

Introduction

I n the software development lifecycle, testing and quality assurance (QA) are crucial components that ensure the reliability, performance, and maintainability of applications. This chapter focuses on the importance of testing in C++, various testing methodologies, frameworks, and tools, as well as best practices for implementing effective testing strategies in scalable software development. By adopting rigorous testing practices, developers can catch bugs early, improve code quality, and ensure that their applications can scale effectively under various conditions.

1. The Importance of Testing in Software Development

1.1. Why Testing Matters

Testing is an integral part of software development, particularly for scalable applications that need to handle increasing loads and complex interactions. Effective testing helps identify and resolve defects early in the development process, reducing the cost of fixing issues and enhancing the overall quality of the product.

- **Benefits of Testing**:
- **Early Bug Detection**: Catching defects during the development phase minimizes the risk of late-stage failures.
- **Improved Code Quality**: Thorough testing encourages developers to write cleaner, more maintainable code.
- **Enhanced User Satisfaction**: Reliable and well-tested applications lead to better user experiences and increased trust.

1.2. Testing as a Continuous Process

In agile and DevOps environments, testing is not a one-time activity but a continuous process integrated into the development lifecycle. Continuous testing helps ensure that each iteration of the software meets the quality standards before deployment.

- **Continuous Integration and Continuous Deployment (CI/CD)**: Implementing CI/CD pipelines allows for automated testing at various stages, ensuring that code changes do not introduce new bugs.

2. Testing Methodologies

2.1. Unit Testing

Unit testing focuses on testing individual components or functions in isolation. This methodology helps verify that each unit of code behaves as expected, making it easier to identify and fix bugs.

- **Key Characteristics of Unit Tests**:
- **Isolation**: Each test should verify one aspect of the unit being tested.
- **Fast Execution**: Unit tests should execute quickly, encouraging frequent testing.
- **Automation**: Unit tests are typically automated to ensure consistent execution.

Example: Using Google Test to implement a unit test for a simple math function.

```cpp
Copy code
#include <gtest/gtest.h>

// Function to be tested
int add(int a, int b) {
    return a + b;
}

// Unit test
TEST(MathTests, Addition) {
    EXPECT_EQ(add(2, 3), 5);
    EXPECT_EQ(add(-1, 1), 0);
}
```

2.2. Integration Testing

Integration testing focuses on verifying the interactions between different components or modules. This methodology ensures that combined parts of the application work together correctly.

- **Types of Integration Testing**:
- **Big Bang Integration**: All components are integrated at once and tested together.
- **Incremental Integration**: Components are integrated and tested one at a time, either top-down or bottom-up.

Example: Testing a module that interacts with a database and verifying that the data is correctly retrieved and stored.

2.3. System Testing

System testing is a high-level testing methodology that validates the complete and integrated software system. It checks the end-to-end functionality of the application against the specified requirements.

- **Types of System Testing**:
- **Functional Testing**: Verifies that the software functions according to the requirements.
- **Non-Functional Testing**: Assesses performance, security, usability, and reliability.

2.4. Acceptance Testing

Acceptance testing is performed to determine whether the system meets the acceptance criteria and is ready for deployment. This testing is usually conducted by end-users or stakeholders.

- **User Acceptance Testing (UAT)**: Involves real users testing the software to ensure it meets their needs and expectations.

3. Testing Frameworks for C++

3.1. Google Test

Google Test is one of the most widely used testing frameworks for C++. It provides a rich set of assertions and test case management, making it easy to write and execute unit tests.

- **Features of Google Test**:
- **Test Fixtures**: Allow the setup of a common environment for related tests.
- **Assertions**: A comprehensive set of assertions for verifying expected outcomes.
- **Mock Objects**: Supports mocking dependencies to isolate units being tested.

Example: Setting up a test fixture in Google Test.

```cpp
Copy code
class MathTest : public ::testing::Test {
protected:
    void SetUp() override {
        // Initialization code
    }

    void TearDown() override {
        // Cleanup code
    }
};

TEST_F(MathTest, Addition) {
    EXPECT_EQ(add(2, 3), 5);
}
```

3.2. Catch2

Catch2 is a lightweight, header-only testing framework that is easy to integrate into C++ projects. It supports both unit and integration testing with a simple syntax.

- **Features of Catch2**:
- **Natural Language Syntax**: Tests are written in a way that is easy to read and understand.
- **Automatic Test Discovery**: Automatically discovers and runs tests without requiring explicit registration.

Example: A simple Catch2 test case.

```cpp
Copy code
#define CATCH_CONFIG_MAIN
#include <catch2/catch.hpp>

TEST_CASE("Addition") {
```

```
    REQUIRE(add(2, 3) == 5);
}
```

3.3. Boost.Test

Boost.Test is part of the Boost C++ Libraries and provides a flexible framework for unit testing. It is feature-rich and supports both simple and complex test scenarios.

- **Features of Boost.Test**:
- **Test Suites**: Organize tests into suites for better management.
- **Fixtures and Hooks**: Support for setup and teardown operations.

Example: Implementing a test case with Boost.Test.

```cpp
Copy code
#define BOOST_TEST_MODULE MyTest
#include <boost/test/included/unit_test.hpp>

BOOST_AUTO_TEST_CASE(addition) {
    BOOST_CHECK(add(2, 3) == 5);
}
```

4. Continuous Integration and Testing

4.1. The Role of CI in Testing

Continuous Integration (CI) is a development practice where code changes are automatically tested and integrated into the main codebase. This process helps ensure that code changes do not introduce new defects.

- **CI Pipeline**: A CI pipeline typically includes stages for building, testing, and deploying code changes.

4.2. Setting Up a CI/CD Pipeline for C++ Projects

- **Tools**: Common CI tools include Jenkins, GitHub Actions, Travis CI, and CircleCI.
- **Configuring the Pipeline**: Outline the steps to set up a CI pipeline that automatically runs tests whenever changes are pushed to the repository.

Example: A simple GitHub Actions configuration file to run tests on every push.

```yaml
Copy code
name: C++ CI

on: [push, pull_request]

jobs:
  build:
    runs-on: ubuntu-latest

    steps:
      - name: Checkout code
        uses: actions/checkout@v2

      - name: Install dependencies
        run: sudo apt-get install -y g++ cmake

      - name: Build
        run: cmake . && make

      - name: Run tests
        run: ./run_tests
```

5. Performance Testing and Benchmarking

5.1. The Importance of Performance Testing

Performance testing ensures that the application can handle expected loads efficiently. It assesses various aspects such as response time, throughput, and resource utilization.

5.2. Benchmarking Techniques

Benchmarking involves measuring the performance of specific code segments to identify bottlenecks and optimize resource usage.

- **Tools for Benchmarking**: Tools like Google Benchmark can be used to perform accurate measurements of function performance.

Example: A simple benchmark using Google Benchmark.

```cpp
Copy code
#include <benchmark/benchmark.h>

static void BM_Add(benchmark::State& state) {
    for (auto _ : state) {
        add(2, 3);
    }
}
BENCHMARK(BM_Add);
```

5.3. Load Testing

Load testing simulates user demand on the application to identify how it performs under high load conditions. This testing helps ensure the application can scale effectively.

- **Tools for Load Testing**: Tools like Apache JMeter or Gatling can simulate high traffic scenarios.

6. Quality Assurance Best Practices

6.1. Writing Testable Code

To facilitate effective testing, writing testable code is essential. This involves structuring the codebase to support easy testing.

- **Principles for Writing Testable Code**:
- **Separation of Concerns**: Ensure components are modular and focused on specific tasks.
- **Dependency Injection**: Use dependency injection to allow easier mocking of dependencies during testing.

6.2. Code Reviews and Static Analysis

Code reviews and static analysis tools help ensure code quality before it enters the testing phase.

- **Static Analysis Tools**: Tools like cppcheck, Clang Static Analyzer, and SonarQube help identify potential issues in the code.

6.3. Documentation and Test Cases

Maintaining clear documentation for both the codebase and test cases is vital for ensuring that tests remain relevant and effective.

- **Documenting Test Cases**: Provide details on the purpose of each test, expected outcomes, and any dependencies.

7. Real-World Case Studies in Testing and Quality Assurance

7.1. Case Study 1: Scalable E-Commerce Platform

Explore how an e-commerce platform implemented robust testing practices, including unit tests, integration tests, and performance testing, to ensure scalability and reliability.

7.2. Case Study 2: Multi-Threaded Game Engine

Analyze how a game engine used various testing methodologies to validate gameplay mechanics, performance, and user interactions, ensuring a seamless gaming experience.

7.3. Case Study 3: Financial Trading System

Examine how a financial trading application employed rigorous testing and quality assurance practices to handle complex algorithms and real-time data processing, maintaining high performance and reliability.

Conclusion

In this chapter, we discussed the critical role of testing and quality assurance in scalable software development using C++. By implementing effective testing methodologies, utilizing robust frameworks, and adopting continuous integration practices, developers can ensure that their applications are reliable, maintainable, and capable of handling increased workloads. Real-world case studies highlighted the practical application of these testing strategies, underscoring their importance in delivering high-quality software. As we continue to explore advanced C++ techniques and architectural patterns, the insights gained from this chapter will be invaluable in building scalable applications.

Chapter 9: Performance Optimization and Profiling Techniques in C++ for Scalable Software Development

Introduction

As software systems grow in complexity and scale, ensuring optimal performance becomes crucial for meeting user demands and providing a seamless experience. Performance optimization involves fine-tuning various aspects of the code, algorithms, and architecture to enhance execution speed, reduce resource usage, and improve responsiveness. This chapter explores advanced performance optimization techniques, profiling tools, and methodologies that are vital for developing high-performance, scalable applications in C++.

1. Understanding Performance Optimization

1.1. What is Performance Optimization?

Performance optimization refers to the process of improving the efficiency of a software application in terms of speed, resource usage, and overall responsiveness. In C++, this often involves analyzing and modifying code, algorithms, and data structures to reduce execution time and memory consumption.

- **Key Aspects of Performance**:
- **Execution Time**: The time taken to execute a task or a series of tasks.
- **Memory Usage**: The amount of memory consumed by the application during its execution.
- **Responsiveness**: The ability of an application to respond quickly to user interactions or events.

1.2. Importance of Performance Optimization

Optimizing performance is essential for several reasons:

- **User Experience**: Users expect applications to be fast and responsive. Slow performance can lead to frustration and disengagement.
- **Scalability**: As user loads increase, optimized applications can handle more requests without degrading performance.
- **Resource Efficiency**: Efficient code reduces resource consumption, leading to lower operational costs and improved sustainability.

2. Performance Profiling Techniques

2.1. What is Profiling?

Profiling is the process of measuring the performance of an application to identify bottlenecks, memory usage patterns, and execution paths. Profiling helps developers understand where the application spends the most time and resources.

2.2. Types of Profiling

- **CPU Profiling**: Measures where the CPU spends its time, helping identify slow functions or methods.
- **Memory Profiling**: Analyzes memory allocation and usage patterns to detect leaks and inefficiencies.
- **I/O Profiling**: Evaluates input/output operations, identifying delays

caused by file or network access.

2.3. Profiling Tools for C++

Several tools can assist in profiling C++ applications, providing insights into performance bottlenecks.

- **gprof**: A GNU profiler that helps analyze performance and execution time of functions in C++ applications.
- **Valgrind**: A powerful tool for detecting memory leaks and profiling memory usage.
- **Perf**: A Linux profiling tool that provides various performance counters and profiling capabilities.
- **Visual Studio Profiler**: Integrated profiling tools for applications developed in Microsoft Visual Studio.

Example: Use gprof to analyze a sample C++ application and identify the slowest functions.

3. Analyzing Performance Bottlenecks

3.1. Identifying Bottlenecks

A bottleneck in software refers to a component that significantly limits performance. Identifying these bottlenecks is crucial for effective optimization.

- **Common Sources of Bottlenecks**:
- **Inefficient Algorithms**: Using algorithms with high time complexity can drastically slow down performance.
- **Excessive Memory Allocations**: Frequent dynamic memory allocations can lead to fragmentation and overhead.
- **Lock Contention**: In multi-threaded applications, contention for locks can reduce throughput and increase latency.

3.2. Using Profiling Results to Optimize

Once bottlenecks are identified through profiling, developers can focus their optimization efforts on these critical areas. This targeted approach ensures that time and resources are spent effectively.

- **Case Study**: Discuss a performance profiling example where a CPU bottleneck was identified in a data processing application, leading to an optimization of the algorithm used.

4. Optimization Techniques

4.1. Algorithmic Optimizations

Choosing the right algorithm can have a significant impact on performance. Understanding algorithm complexity is essential for optimizing performance.

- **Big O Notation**: A notation that describes the performance or complexity of an algorithm in terms of time and space. It's crucial to evaluate algorithms to choose the most efficient ones for the task.
- **Example**: Compare the performance of linear search versus binary search on sorted datasets.

4.2. Code Optimizations

In addition to selecting efficient algorithms, developers can apply various code-level optimizations.

- **Inlining Functions**: Using the inline keyword can reduce function call overhead for small, frequently called functions.

Example:

```cpp
Copy code
```

```
inline int square(int x) {
    return x * x;
}
```

- **Loop Optimizations**: Techniques such as loop unrolling can reduce overhead in performance-critical loops.

Example:

```cpp
Copy code
for (int i = 0; i < n; i += 4) {
    // Process four elements in one iteration
}
```

4.3. Memory Management Optimizations

Memory allocation and deallocation can introduce overhead, particularly in high-performance applications. Optimizing memory usage is crucial.

- **Pooling and Object Reuse**: Implementing object pools can reduce the overhead of frequent allocations.

Example: Create a simple object pool for managing a set of objects efficiently.

- **Cache Locality**: Designing data structures to maximize cache usage can significantly improve performance.

Example: Use contiguous memory storage (like std::vector) to improve cache hits compared to linked structures.

4.4. Concurrency Optimizations

For multi-threaded applications, optimizations can enhance parallel performance and resource usage.

- **Minimizing Lock Contention**: Use finer-grained locks or lock-free data structures to reduce contention among threads.
- **Thread Pooling**: Reusing threads can minimize the overhead associated with thread creation and destruction.

5. Advanced Optimization Techniques

5.1. Compiler Optimization Flags

Using compiler optimization flags can enhance performance without altering the source code.

- **Common Optimization Flags**:
- -O1, -O2, -O3: Levels of optimization that enable different compiler optimizations.
- -march=native: Optimizes code for the architecture of the host machine.

Example: Compile a C++ program with various optimization flags and compare performance.

5.2. Profile-Guided Optimization (PGO)

Profile-Guided Optimization involves collecting profiling data during the execution of the program and using that data to guide optimizations in subsequent compilations.

- **Process**:
- Compile the program with instrumentation to gather performance data.
- Execute the instrumented program with representative workloads.
- Recompile the program using the collected profile data to optimize performance.

6. Best Practices for Performance Optimization

6.1. Measure Before You Optimize

Always measure performance before making optimizations. Premature optimization can lead to wasted effort and unnecessary complexity.

- **Tools for Measurement**: Utilize profiling tools to gather accurate performance data.

6.2. Optimize for Readability and Maintainability

While optimizing for performance, maintain readability and maintainability. Highly optimized code can become difficult to understand and maintain.

- **Balancing Optimization and Clarity**: Document any performance optimizations thoroughly to ensure that future developers understand the reasoning behind them.

6.3. Continuous Profiling and Monitoring

In a production environment, continuously monitor application performance to identify potential bottlenecks as the codebase evolves.

- **Tools for Monitoring**: Use application performance monitoring (APM) tools like New Relic or Datadog to monitor runtime performance metrics.

7. Real-World Case Studies: Performance Optimization in Action

7.1. Case Study 1: High-Performance Image Processing Application

Examine how an image processing application used performance profiling to identify bottlenecks in its algorithms, leading to significant optimizations and improved throughput.

- **Techniques Used**: Algorithmic improvements, memory pooling, and cache optimization.

7.2. Case Study 2: Scalable Web Application

Explore how a scalable web application implemented continuous profiling and optimization techniques to handle increased traffic while maintaining response times.

- **Challenges and Solutions**: Discuss the strategies used to improve database access patterns and reduce latency.

7.3. Case Study 3: Real-Time Analytics Platform

Analyze a real-time analytics platform that utilized advanced C++ techniques and optimizations to process large volumes of data quickly and efficiently.

- **Optimizations Implemented**: Profile-guided optimization, multi-threaded data processing, and efficient memory management.

Conclusion

In this chapter, we explored performance optimization and profiling techniques essential for scalable software development in C++. By understanding the principles of optimization, utilizing advanced techniques, and employing effective profiling tools, developers can create applications that perform efficiently under varying loads. The real-world case studies illustrated how these techniques can be applied in practice, providing valuable insights into the optimization process. As we move forward, the skills gained in this chapter will serve as a foundation for implementing robust, high-performance C++ applications.

Chapter 10: Best Practices in Software Development for C++ and Scalability

Introduction

I n the dynamic world of software development, adhering to best practices is crucial for building robust, maintainable, and scalable applications. This chapter discusses essential best practices in C++ programming that foster clean code, facilitate collaboration, and ensure scalability. By implementing these practices, developers can enhance the quality of their codebases and prepare their applications for future growth and complexity. We will cover coding standards, architectural principles, testing methodologies, and more, providing practical insights into how these elements contribute to scalable software development.

1. Coding Standards and Style Guides

1.1. Importance of Coding Standards

Coding standards establish a set of guidelines for writing code, promoting consistency and readability across a codebase. Consistent code helps team members understand each other's work more easily and facilitates collaboration.

- **Key Benefits**:
- **Improved Readability**: Well-structured code is easier to read and understand.
- **Reduced Errors**: Following standards can minimize common coding mistakes.
- **Enhanced Collaboration**: Team members can contribute more effectively to the codebase.

1.2. Common Coding Standards for C++

Many organizations adopt specific coding standards to maintain code quality. Notable standards include:

- **Google C++ Style Guide**: Emphasizes readability, clear naming conventions, and consistent formatting.
- **C++ Core Guidelines**: A set of guidelines for safe and efficient C++ programming, focusing on modern practices.

Example Expansion: Outline key style guide elements, such as naming conventions (e.g., CamelCase for classes, snake_case for functions) and indentation rules.

1.3. Code Review Practices

Regular code reviews are essential for maintaining code quality and ensuring adherence to coding standards. They provide an opportunity for team members to offer feedback and identify potential issues early in the development process.

- **Best Practices for Code Reviews**:
- **Establish Clear Guidelines**: Define what to look for during reviews (e.g., adherence to coding standards, logic errors, performance considerations).
- **Focus on Constructive Feedback**: Encourage a positive environment that promotes learning and improvement.

2. Principles of Software Architecture

2.1. The Role of Software Architecture

Software architecture defines the structure and organization of a system, influencing its performance, maintainability, and scalability. A well-thought-out architecture serves as a blueprint for the entire application, guiding the development process.

- **Key Architectural Concepts**:
- **Modularity**: Dividing the system into independent modules to enhance maintainability and scalability.
- **Loose Coupling**: Reducing dependencies between components to allow for easier changes and upgrades.
- **High Cohesion**: Ensuring that each module or component has a single, well-defined responsibility.

2.2. Common Architectural Patterns

Adopting established architectural patterns can significantly improve the scalability of C++ applications.

- **Layered Architecture**: Organizes the system into layers (presentation, business logic, data access) to separate concerns.
- **Microservices Architecture**: Decomposes the application into small, independently deployable services, allowing for scalable deployment and development.
- **Event-Driven Architecture**: Promotes asynchronous communication between components, enhancing scalability and responsiveness.

Example: Provide an overview of a microservices architecture implemented for an e-commerce platform, highlighting the advantages of scalability and modularity.

3. Effective Use of Modern C++ Features

3.1. Leveraging Smart Pointers

Modern C++ introduces smart pointers, which help manage memory more effectively and reduce the risk of memory leaks.

- **Types of Smart Pointers**:
- **std::unique_ptr**: Ensures exclusive ownership of a dynamically allocated object.
- **std::shared_ptr**: Allows shared ownership among multiple pointers.
- **std::weak_ptr**: Prevents circular references when using shared pointers.

Example Expansion: Illustrate the usage of smart pointers in a C++ application and compare it with traditional raw pointer management.

3.2. Utilizing Standard Libraries

The C++ Standard Library provides a wealth of tools and functions that can simplify common programming tasks.

- **Benefits of Using Standard Libraries**:
- **Reduced Development Time**: Leverage existing, tested solutions instead of reinventing the wheel.
- **Performance**: Standard libraries are optimized for performance and often leverage advanced algorithms and data structures.
- **Common Libraries**:
- **STL (Standard Template Library)**: Provides generic classes and functions for data structures and algorithms.
- **Boost Libraries**: A collection of peer-reviewed libraries that extend C++ capabilities.

4. Testing Methodologies for C++ Applications

4.1. Importance of Testing
Testing is a critical part of the software development process, ensuring that the application functions correctly and meets user requirements.

- **Key Benefits**:
- **Early Bug Detection**: Identifying issues early saves time and resources.
- **Increased Confidence**: A robust testing suite increases confidence in code changes.

4.2. Types of Testing
Various testing methodologies can be applied to C++ applications to ensure quality.

- **Unit Testing**: Focuses on testing individual components or functions in isolation.
- **Integration Testing**: Validates the interactions between different components.
- **System Testing**: Tests the complete and integrated system to ensure it meets requirements.
- **User Acceptance Testing (UAT)**: Involves end-users testing the application to confirm it meets their needs.

Example: Use Google Test to illustrate unit testing for a C++ function.

4.3. Test-Driven Development (TDD)
Test-Driven Development emphasizes writing tests before the actual code. This approach helps clarify requirements and leads to better design.

- **TDD Cycle**:

1. Write a failing test.
2. Write the minimal code to pass the test.

3. Refactor the code while keeping the tests green.

5. Performance Optimization Techniques

5.1. Understanding Performance Bottlenecks

Identifying performance bottlenecks is essential for effective optimization. Common sources include inefficient algorithms, excessive memory allocations, and lock contention in multi-threaded applications.

5.2. Profiling Tools

Profiling tools help developers analyze performance and identify bottlenecks.

- **Common Profiling Tools**:
- **gprof**: A GNU profiler that provides insights into function call performance.
- **Valgrind**: Detects memory leaks and provides profiling capabilities.
- **Perf**: A Linux tool for profiling applications with various performance counters.

Example: Profile a simple C++ application using gprof to identify slow functions.

5.3. Optimization Strategies

- **Algorithmic Improvements**: Choosing efficient algorithms is critical. Evaluate time complexity and choose the best algorithm for the task.
- **Memory Management**: Minimize dynamic memory allocations and consider using object pools for frequently created and destroyed objects.
- **Compiler Optimizations**: Utilize compiler flags (e.g., -O2, -O3) to enable various optimizations during compilation.

6. Documentation and Code Quality

6.1. The Role of Documentation

Good documentation is essential for maintaining a clean codebase. It helps new team members understand the code and provides insights into design decisions.

6.2. Best Practices for Documentation

- **Code Comments**: Use comments to explain complex logic and document the "why" behind decisions rather than the "what."
- **API Documentation**: Maintain comprehensive documentation for APIs, including usage examples and explanations of parameters.

6.3. Static Analysis Tools

Static analysis tools help identify potential issues in the code before runtime.

- **Common Static Analysis Tools**:
- **cppcheck**: A static analysis tool for C++ code that detects various issues.
- **Clang Static Analyzer**: Provides static analysis for C/C++ codebases, identifying bugs and vulnerabilities.

7. Continuous Integration and Deployment

7.1. The Importance of CI/CD

Continuous Integration (CI) and Continuous Deployment (CD) are practices that help automate the testing and deployment processes. These practices ensure that code changes are integrated and deployed frequently, reducing the risk of bugs and improving release cycles.

7.2. Setting Up a CI/CD Pipeline

Implementing a CI/CD pipeline involves several steps:

- **Choosing a CI/CD Tool**: Tools like Jenkins, GitHub Actions, and GitLab

CI can automate the build, test, and deployment processes.

- **Configuring the Pipeline**: Define steps for building, testing, and deploying the application.

Example: Provide a sample GitHub Actions configuration file that builds and tests a C++ application on each push.

```yaml
Copy code
name: C++ CI

on: [push, pull_request]

jobs:
  build:
    runs-on: ubuntu-latest

    steps:
      - name: Checkout code
        uses: actions/checkout@v2

      - name: Install dependencies
        run: sudo apt-get install -y g++ cmake

      - name: Build
        run: cmake . && make

      - name: Run tests
        run: ./run_tests
```

8. Case Studies in C++ Development

8.1. Case Study 1: Scalable E-Commerce Platform

Explore how an e-commerce platform implemented best practices in coding standards, testing methodologies, and performance optimization to handle increased traffic and complexity.

8.2. Case Study 2: High-Performance Game Engine

Analyze how a game engine utilized modern C++ features, rigorous testing, and performance profiling to deliver an engaging and responsive gaming experience.

8.3. Case Study 3: Real-Time Financial Trading System

Examine a financial trading application that adopted continuous integration and robust testing practices to ensure high reliability and performance under demanding conditions.

Conclusion

In this chapter, we explored best practices for software development in C++ that promote scalability, maintainability, and performance. By adhering to coding standards, implementing effective testing methodologies, optimizing performance, and embracing continuous integration, developers can build robust applications that meet user demands and adapt to changing requirements. The insights gained from real-world case studies demonstrate the practical application of these best practices, providing a foundation for future development endeavors. As we continue to advance in C++ and software engineering practices, these principles will remain critical to achieving scalable and high-quality software solutions.

Chapter 11: Leveraging C++ for Cross-Platform Development and Scalability

Introduction

Cross-platform development is an essential aspect of modern software engineering, allowing applications to run on various operating systems and devices. C++ is particularly well-suited for cross-platform development due to its performance, efficiency, and the ability to interface with low-level system resources. This chapter delves into strategies, tools, and best practices for leveraging C++ to create scalable, cross-platform applications. We will explore how to manage platform-specific code, utilize libraries and frameworks, and optimize performance across different environments.

1. Understanding Cross-Platform Development

1.1. What is Cross-Platform Development?

Cross-platform development refers to the practice of writing software applications that can run on multiple operating systems and environments without significant modification. This approach increases the reach of applications and can significantly reduce development time and costs.

- **Benefits of Cross-Platform Development**:
- **Wider Audience Reach**: Applications can cater to users across different operating systems, such as Windows, macOS, and Linux.
- **Reduced Development Time**: A single codebase can be maintained for multiple platforms, streamlining the development process.
- **Consistency**: Users experience a similar interface and functionality regardless of the platform.

1.2. Challenges of Cross-Platform Development

While cross-platform development offers numerous advantages, it also presents challenges, including:

- **Platform-Specific Differences**: Different operating systems have varying APIs, UI conventions, and performance characteristics that must be managed.
- **Performance Overhead**: Abstraction layers can introduce performance penalties compared to native applications.
- **Testing Complexity**: Testing across multiple platforms can complicate the development process, requiring comprehensive testing strategies.

2. C++: A Strong Candidate for Cross-Platform Development

2.1. Performance and Efficiency

C++ is known for its high performance and efficiency, making it an ideal choice for resource-intensive applications. It allows developers to write low-level code that interacts directly with hardware while still providing high-level abstractions.

- **Optimized Resource Management**: C++ provides direct control over memory management, enabling developers to optimize resource usage effectively.

2.2. Extensive Standard Library Support

The C++ Standard Library offers a rich set of features, including data structures, algorithms, and input/output facilities, which are consistent across platforms.

- **Boost Libraries**: The Boost C++ Libraries provide additional functionality that is also cross-platform, extending the capabilities of standard C++.

2.3. Community and Ecosystem

C++ has a vast ecosystem of libraries, frameworks, and tools that support cross-platform development. The active community contributes to the continuous improvement and evolution of the language.

3. Tools and Frameworks for Cross-Platform Development in C++

3.1. CMake

CMake is a cross-platform build system that simplifies the process of managing project builds across different platforms. It allows developers to define the build process in a platform-independent way.

- **Key Features of CMake**:
- **Cross-Platform Support**: Automatically generates build files for different platforms (Makefiles, Visual Studio projects, etc.).
- **Out-of-Source Builds**: Supports building in a separate directory, keeping the source tree clean.

Example: A simple CMakeLists.txt file for a C++ project.

```cmake
Copy code
cmake_minimum_required(VERSION 3.10)
project(MyProject)
```

```
set(CMAKE_CXX_STANDARD 11)

add_executable(MyExecutable main.cpp)
```

3.2. Qt Framework

Qt is a powerful framework for developing cross-platform applications with a rich set of features, including UI components, networking, and file handling.

- **Benefits of Using Qt**:
- **Cross-Platform GUI Development**: Qt provides tools for creating graphical user interfaces that work on multiple platforms.
- **Integrated Tools**: Qt Creator IDE simplifies the development process with debugging, profiling, and design tools.

Example: Creating a simple Qt application.

```cpp
Copy code
#include <QApplication>
#include <QPushButton>

int main(int argc, char *argv[]) {
    QApplication app(argc, argv);
    QPushButton button("Hello, World!");
    button.show();
    return app.exec();
}
```

3.3. wxWidgets

wxWidgets is another popular cross-platform GUI library for C++. It allows developers to create native applications for various platforms with a single codebase.

- **Key Features**:
- **Native Look and Feel**: wxWidgets applications have the native appearance and behavior on each platform.
- **Extensive Widget Library**: Offers a wide range of UI components and tools.

4. Managing Platform-Specific Code

4.1. Conditional Compilation
Conditional compilation allows developers to include or exclude parts of the code based on the platform or environment.

- **Using Preprocessor Directives**: C++ preprocessor directives (#ifdef, #ifndef, #define, #endif) help manage platform-specific code.

Example:

```cpp
Copy code
#ifdef _WIN32
#include <windows.h>
#else
#include <unistd.h>
#endif
```

4.2. Abstracting Platform-Specific Functionality
Creating abstractions for platform-specific features can help manage differences between platforms without scattering conditional code throughout the application.

- **Using Interfaces**: Define interfaces for platform-specific functionalities and provide concrete implementations for each platform.

Example:

```cpp
Copy code
class PlatformInterface {
public:
    virtual void performOperation() = 0;
};

class WindowsPlatform : public PlatformInterface {
public:
    void performOperation() override {
        // Windows-specific implementation
    }
};

class LinuxPlatform : public PlatformInterface {
public:
    void performOperation() override {
        // Linux-specific implementation
    }
};
```

4.3. Testing on Multiple Platforms

Ensuring that the application works correctly across different platforms requires thorough testing.

- **Setting Up a Cross-Platform Test Environment**: Use CI/CD tools to automate testing on various platforms, ensuring consistent behavior and performance.

5. Performance Considerations in Cross-Platform Development

5.1. Platform-Specific Optimizations

Different platforms may have distinct performance characteristics. Understanding these can help optimize applications for each environment.

- **Windows vs. Linux Performance**: Analyze how system calls, threading models, and resource management differ between Windows and Linux, and how to optimize for each.

5.2. Resource Management

Efficient resource management is crucial for performance, especially in cross-platform applications that may run in resource-constrained environments.

- **Managing Memory**: Use smart pointers and custom allocators to handle memory efficiently across different platforms.

5.3. Profiling Across Platforms

Profiling tools vary by platform, but using cross-platform profiling tools allows you to analyze performance consistently.

- **Tools**: Mention profiling tools that work across platforms, such as Valgrind, gprof, and Intel VTune.

6. Best Practices for Cross-Platform Development in C++

6.1. Code Reusability and Modularity

Designing code for reusability and modularity can simplify cross-platform development.

- **Modular Architecture**: Use a modular approach to separate platform-independent and platform-specific code, facilitating easier maintenance and updates.

6.2. Leveraging Existing Libraries

Utilizing well-established libraries that support cross-platform functionality can save development time and enhance application quality.

- **Example Libraries**: Qt, Boost, and OpenCV are excellent choices for cross-platform functionality.

6.3. Documentation and Collaboration
Maintaining clear documentation and fostering collaboration within the development team are critical for successful cross-platform projects.

- **Documentation**: Ensure that the project documentation includes details on how to build and run the application on different platforms.
- **Collaboration Tools**: Use version control systems (e.g., Git) and collaborative tools (e.g., Jira, Confluence) to manage project workflows effectively.

7. Real-World Case Studies in Cross-Platform C++ Development

7.1. Case Study 1: Cross-Platform Game Development
Examine how a game development studio leveraged C++ to create a cross-platform game, discussing the challenges faced and solutions implemented.

- **Key Takeaways**: Highlight the use of libraries, performance optimizations, and testing strategies.

7.2. Case Study 2: Scalable IoT Applications
Analyze how a company developed an IoT application using C++ to work across various devices and platforms, ensuring scalability and performance.

- **Challenges and Solutions**: Discuss the integration of hardware communication protocols and performance optimizations for limited-resource devices.

7.3. Case Study 3: Financial Software Across Platforms
Explore a financial software application that utilized C++ for cross-platform support, focusing on performance, security, and compliance with financial regulations.

Conclusion

In this chapter, we explored the essentials of cross-platform development in C++, focusing on strategies, tools, and best practices to ensure scalability and performance. C++ offers powerful capabilities for building cross-platform applications, but it also requires careful management of platform-specific code and thorough testing. By adopting the techniques discussed, developers can create high-quality applications that cater to a diverse user base while maintaining efficiency and responsiveness. As we continue to delve deeper into advanced C++ techniques, the insights gained in this chapter will be invaluable for building scalable and maintainable software solutions.

Chapter 12: C++ in Cloud Computing: Scalability, Performance, and Best Practices

Introduction

C loud computing has revolutionized how software applications are developed, deployed, and scaled. By leveraging the power of the cloud, developers can create applications that are not only highly available but also capable of handling massive workloads. C++ plays a vital role in cloud computing, offering the performance and efficiency needed for resource-intensive applications. This chapter explores the advantages of using C++ in cloud environments, the frameworks and tools available, best practices for development, and real-world applications of C++ in cloud computing.

1. Understanding Cloud Computing

1.1. What is Cloud Computing?

Cloud computing is the delivery of computing services over the internet, allowing users to access and store data on remote servers instead of local machines. The primary models of cloud computing include:

- **Infrastructure as a Service (IaaS)**: Provides virtualized computing resources over the internet (e.g., AWS EC2, Google Cloud Compute).
- **Platform as a Service (PaaS)**: Offers a platform allowing developers to build, deploy, and manage applications without dealing with the underlying infrastructure (e.g., Heroku, Google App Engine).
- **Software as a Service (SaaS)**: Delivers software applications over the internet on a subscription basis (e.g., Microsoft Office 365, Salesforce).

1.2. Benefits of Cloud Computing

- **Scalability**: Easily scale resources up or down based on demand.
- **Cost-Effectiveness**: Pay for only the resources used, reducing capital expenses.
- **Flexibility**: Access applications and data from anywhere, enabling remote work and collaboration.

2. C++: A Strong Candidate for Cloud Applications

2.1. Performance and Efficiency

C++ is known for its high performance and low-level control, making it suitable for cloud applications that require efficient resource management. Applications that need to process large amounts of data or require real-time processing can benefit significantly from C++.

- **Low Latency**: C++ applications can achieve lower latency compared to higher-level languages, which is critical for performance-sensitive applications.

2.2. System-Level Access

C++ provides system-level access, allowing developers to optimize network operations, memory management, and threading models that are essential in cloud environments.

- **Network Programming**: C++ offers libraries like Boost.Asio for asynchronous I/O, which is crucial for building responsive cloud services.

2.3. Rich Ecosystem

C++ has a robust ecosystem of libraries and frameworks that can enhance cloud application development.

- **Boost**: Provides a wide array of libraries for tasks such as multithreading, networking, and data structures.
- **Qt**: Can be used for developing cross-platform cloud applications with a graphical user interface.

3. Developing Cloud Applications with C++

3.1. Frameworks for Cloud Development

Several frameworks facilitate C++ development for cloud applications, enabling developers to build scalable and efficient services.

- **Google Cloud C++ Client Library**: A library that allows developers to interact with Google Cloud services using C++.
- **AWS SDK for C++**: Provides a C++ interface for AWS services, making it easier to integrate C++ applications with AWS resources.
- **Pistache**: A modern and lightweight HTTP server framework for C++, suitable for building RESTful APIs.

Example: Building a simple REST API using Pistache.

```cpp
Copy code
#include <pistache/endpoint.h>

using namespace Pistache;
```

```
class HelloHandler : public Http::Handler {
public:
    HTTP_PROTOTYPE(HelloHandler)

    void onRequest(const Http::Request& request,
    Http::ResponseWriter response) override {
        response.send(Http::Code::Ok, "Hello, World!");
    }
};

int main() {
    Http::Endpoint server(Address(Ipv4::any(), Port(9080)));
    server.init();
    server.setHandler(Http::make_handler<HelloHandler>());
    server.serve();
    return 0;
}
```

3.2. Microservices Architecture

Cloud applications often employ microservices architecture to build scalable and resilient systems. C++ is well-suited for microservices due to its performance characteristics and ability to handle concurrent operations.

- **Advantages of Microservices**:
- **Independently Deployable**: Each service can be developed, deployed, and scaled independently.
- **Technology Agnostic**: Different services can use different technologies and languages, allowing flexibility.

Example: Describe how a C++ microservice can interact with other services written in different languages (e.g., Python, Java).

4. Performance Optimization in Cloud Applications

4.1. Profiling Tools for Cloud Applications

Profiling is essential for understanding how C++ applications perform in the cloud. Several tools can help identify performance bottlenecks.

- **Valgrind**: A tool for memory profiling and detecting memory leaks.
- **gprof**: A GNU profiler that provides function call statistics.
- **Perf**: A Linux profiling tool that offers various performance counters.

Example: Use Valgrind to profile a C++ application and analyze memory usage.

4.2. Network Optimization

Network performance is critical in cloud applications. Optimizing network communication can significantly improve the responsiveness of cloud services.

- **Asynchronous I/O**: Use libraries like Boost.Asio to implement asynchronous network operations, reducing latency.
- **Batch Processing**: Sending data in batches instead of individual requests can improve efficiency.

Example: Compare synchronous versus asynchronous network calls in a cloud service context.

4.3. Resource Management

Efficient resource management is vital for cloud applications, especially under variable load conditions.

- **Scaling Strategies**: Implement horizontal scaling to add more instances of services as demand increases.
- **Load Balancing**: Use load balancers to distribute incoming traffic across multiple instances of services.

5. Security Considerations in Cloud Development

5.1. Securing C++ Applications in the Cloud

Security is a critical aspect of cloud applications. Developers must implement robust security measures to protect sensitive data and ensure compliance with regulations.

- **Data Encryption**: Use encryption libraries (e.g., OpenSSL) to secure data in transit and at rest.
- **Authentication and Authorization**: Implement secure authentication mechanisms, such as OAuth or JWT, to control access to services.

5.2. Security Best Practices

- **Input Validation**: Always validate inputs to prevent injection attacks.
- **Regular Security Audits**: Conduct regular audits and vulnerability assessments to identify and address potential security issues.

6. Continuous Integration and Deployment in Cloud Environments

6.1. Importance of CI/CD

Continuous Integration (CI) and Continuous Deployment (CD) practices are crucial for maintaining high-quality cloud applications. These practices allow for automated testing and deployment, ensuring that code changes are thoroughly validated.

- **Benefits of CI/CD**:
- **Rapid Feedback**: Developers receive immediate feedback on code changes, enabling quick fixes.
- **Consistent Releases**: Automating deployment ensures that the release process is repeatable and consistent.

6.2. Setting Up CI/CD for C++ Applications

- **Tools for CI/CD**: Common tools include Jenkins, GitHub Actions, GitLab CI, and CircleCI.

Example: Configure a CI/CD pipeline using GitHub Actions to automate testing and deployment of a C++ cloud application.

```yaml
yaml
Copy code
name: C++ CI

on: [push, pull_request]

jobs:
  build:
    runs-on: ubuntu-latest

    steps:
      - name: Checkout code
        uses: actions/checkout@v2

      - name: Install dependencies
        run: sudo apt-get install -y g++ cmake

      - name: Build
        run: cmake . && make

      - name: Run tests
        run: ./run_tests
```

7. Real-World Applications of C++ in Cloud Computing

7.1. Case Study 1: High-Performance Data Analytics Platform

Examine how a data analytics platform leverages C++ to process vast amounts of data in the cloud, utilizing parallel processing and efficient resource management.

7.2. Case Study 2: Cross-Platform Game Server

Analyze how a gaming company developed a cross-platform game server using C++, focusing on scalability, performance optimization, and real-time processing.

7.3. Case Study 3: Financial Trading System in the Cloud

Explore how a financial trading application utilizes C++ in a cloud environment to handle high-frequency trading with minimal latency.

8. Best Practices for C++ Cloud Development

8.1. Write Modular Code

Designing modular code enhances maintainability and scalability. Each module should have a single responsibility and interact with other modules through well-defined interfaces.

8.2. Implement Robust Testing Strategies

Testing is crucial for cloud applications. Adopt comprehensive testing strategies, including unit tests, integration tests, and load tests, to ensure reliability.

8.3. Monitor and Optimize Continuously

Use monitoring tools to keep track of application performance in real-time. Continuous optimization based on performance data helps maintain responsiveness and efficiency.

Conclusion

In this chapter, we explored the role of C++ in cloud computing, emphasizing its strengths in performance, scalability, and efficiency. By leveraging C++'s capabilities and employing best practices in development, testing, and deployment, developers can create robust cloud applications that meet modern user demands. Real-world case studies demonstrated the practical application of these principles, providing insights into how C++ can effectively be used in cloud environments. As cloud computing continues to evolve, the knowledge gained from this chapter will be invaluable for building future-ready applications.

Chapter 13: Future Trends in C++ Development and Scalability

Introduction

C++ has long been a cornerstone of high-performance software development, providing the power and efficiency required for a wide array of applications, from operating systems to game engines. As technology evolves, so too does the C++ language and its ecosystem. This chapter explores future trends in C++ development, focusing on advancements in the language itself, evolving programming paradigms, and the implications for scalability and performance in software applications. By understanding these trends, developers can better prepare for the future of C++ and harness its potential to build robust, scalable systems.

1. Evolving C++ Language Features

1.1. C++20 and Beyond

C++20 introduced several significant enhancements that streamline development, improve performance, and enhance code readability. Understanding these features is essential for leveraging the full power of modern C++.

- **Modules**: Modules improve compilation times and manage dependencies more effectively by allowing developers to group related code into modules.

Example:

```cpp
Copy code
// Module interface
module math; // Declare a module

export int add(int a, int b) {
    return a + b;
}
```

- **Coroutines**: Coroutines simplify asynchronous programming by allowing functions to pause and resume execution, which is beneficial for scalable applications that rely on concurrency.

Example:

```cpp
Copy code
#include <coroutine>

struct Awaiter {
    bool await_ready() { return false; }
    void await_suspend(std::coroutine_handle<>) {}
    void await_resume() {}
};

co_await Awaiter(); // Using a coroutine
```

- **Concepts**: Concepts enable better type constraints, improving template programming by allowing more expressive and readable code.

Example:

```cpp
Copy code
template<typename T>
concept Incrementable = requires(T x) { ++x; };

template<Incrementable T>
void increment(T& x) {
    ++x;
}
```

1.2. Anticipated Features in C++23 and C++26

Future versions of C++ (C++23 and beyond) are expected to introduce additional features that further enhance the language's capabilities.

- **Pattern Matching**: C++23 is rumored to introduce pattern matching, which simplifies the handling of complex data structures.
- **Static Reflection**: This feature is anticipated to allow developers to introspect and manipulate types at compile time, enhancing metaprogramming capabilities.

2. Emphasis on Performance and Efficiency

2.1. Compiler Optimizations

As compilers evolve, new optimization techniques become available, significantly impacting application performance. Developers should stay informed about advancements in compiler technology to fully exploit these optimizations.

- **Profile-Guided Optimization (PGO)**: Compilers will increasingly support PGO, allowing the compiler to make informed decisions based on profiling data collected during program execution.
- **Link-Time Optimization (LTO)**: LTO allows compilers to optimize across translation units, leading to more efficient executables.

Example: Discuss how to enable PGO and LTO in popular compilers like GCC and Clang.

2.2. Efficient Resource Management

Resource management will continue to be a focus in C++ development, particularly in environments where performance is critical.

- **Improved Memory Models**: Future C++ standards may introduce more sophisticated memory models and features to reduce memory fragmentation and overhead.
- **Smart Resource Management**: Continued emphasis on smart pointers and RAII (Resource Acquisition Is Initialization) principles will help developers write safer, more efficient code.

3. Trends in Concurrency and Parallelism

3.1. Enhanced Concurrency Models

Concurrency is a key aspect of scalable applications. Future trends are likely to introduce more intuitive and efficient concurrency models.

- **Structured Concurrency**: This paradigm aims to simplify the management of concurrent tasks by ensuring that lifetimes are tied to the scope in which they are created, making it easier to reason about the behavior of concurrent code.

3.2. Integration with Hardware Acceleration

As hardware capabilities evolve, C++ will increasingly integrate with hardware acceleration technologies such as GPUs and specialized processors.

- **CUDA and OpenCL**: Leveraging parallel processing capabilities of GPUs through CUDA or OpenCL can significantly enhance performance in compute-intensive applications.
- **SIMD (Single Instruction, Multiple Data)**: Future C++ versions may provide enhanced support for SIMD operations, allowing developers to

exploit vectorization techniques more easily.

4. Growing Ecosystem and Libraries

4.1. Popular C++ Libraries for Modern Development
As C++ continues to evolve, a growing ecosystem of libraries enhances its capabilities, especially for scalable applications.

- **Boost Libraries**: Boost continues to evolve, providing a wide array of libraries that address various programming challenges, including smart pointers, multithreading, and networking.
- **WebAssembly**: C++ is increasingly used with WebAssembly (Wasm) to enable high-performance applications in the browser, expanding the reach of C++ applications to the web.

Example: Discuss how to compile a C++ application to WebAssembly and the implications for cross-platform deployment.

4.2. Rise of C++ in AI and Machine Learning
C++ is gaining traction in the fields of artificial intelligence and machine learning due to its performance advantages.

- **Libraries for AI/ML**: Libraries like TensorFlow and PyTorch have C++ APIs, allowing developers to implement high-performance machine learning models.

5. DevOps and Continuous Deployment in C++

5.1. The Role of DevOps in C++ Development
DevOps practices are increasingly important for ensuring rapid delivery and high quality in software development. This includes automation, continuous integration, and continuous deployment (CI/CD).

- **CI/CD Pipelines**: Implementing CI/CD pipelines allows for automated testing and deployment, ensuring that code changes are consistently validated.

Example: Provide an example of a CI/CD pipeline for a C++ application using GitHub Actions or Jenkins.

5.2. Monitoring and Observability

As applications move to the cloud, monitoring and observability become critical for maintaining performance and reliability.

- **Tools for Monitoring**: Discuss tools like Prometheus, Grafana, and New Relic that can be used to monitor C++ applications in production environments.

6. Security in C++ Applications

6.1. Growing Security Concerns

As applications become more complex and interconnected, security becomes a paramount concern in software development.

- **Common Security Vulnerabilities**: Address vulnerabilities specific to C++, such as buffer overflows, memory leaks, and improper resource management.

6.2. Best Practices for Secure C++ Development

- **Input Validation**: Always validate user input to prevent injection attacks and buffer overflows.
- **Use of Modern C++ Features**: Take advantage of modern C++ features that enhance safety, such as smart pointers and type-safe containers.

7. Real-World Applications and Case Studies

7.1. Case Study 1: Scalable Web Service Architecture
Examine how a tech company utilized C++ to develop a scalable web service architecture that efficiently handles thousands of concurrent users.

7.2. Case Study 2: Cloud-Based Video Processing
Explore a cloud-based video processing platform that leverages C++ for real-time processing and transcoding, discussing the performance optimizations implemented.

7.3. Case Study 3: IoT Device Management
Analyze how C++ is employed in a scalable IoT device management solution, focusing on resource management and connectivity across various devices.

8. Preparing for the Future of C++ Development

8.1. Continuous Learning and Adaptation
As the C++ landscape evolves, developers must stay informed about new features, best practices, and industry trends. Continuous learning is essential for maintaining relevance in the field.

- **Engagement with the Community**: Participate in forums, attend conferences, and contribute to open-source projects to stay connected with the C++ community.

8.2. Embracing New Paradigms
Developers should be open to embracing new programming paradigms and methodologies that enhance scalability and performance.

- **Functional Programming in C++**: While primarily an object-oriented language, C++ supports functional programming techniques that can lead to cleaner and more maintainable code.

8.3. Building a Strong Foundation

Focus on building a strong foundation in C++ principles, data structures, and algorithms. This foundational knowledge is essential for tackling complex software development challenges.

Conclusion

In this chapter, we explored the future trends in C++ development, highlighting advancements in language features, performance optimization techniques, and the growing ecosystem of libraries and tools. As C++ continues to adapt to the evolving landscape of software development, developers must embrace these changes and leverage the power of C++ to build scalable and high-performance applications. The insights gained from real-world case studies demonstrate the practical application of these trends, providing valuable lessons for future development endeavors. By preparing for the future of C++, developers can ensure that their skills remain relevant and that their applications thrive in an increasingly complex technological landscape.

Chapter 14: Case Studies in C++ Development: Success Stories and Lessons Learned

Introduction

C++ has been a cornerstone in software development across various industries, from gaming to finance and cloud computing. This chapter presents a series of case studies showcasing successful C++ implementations in real-world applications. Each case study explores the challenges faced, the strategies employed, and the outcomes achieved. By examining these success stories, we can glean valuable insights and lessons that can guide future C++ development efforts, especially concerning scalability and performance.

1. Case Study 1: High-Performance Game Engine Development

1.1. Overview

In the gaming industry, performance is paramount. A leading game development company aimed to create a high-performance game engine capable of handling complex graphics and physics simulations for AAA titles. The choice of C++ was driven by its efficiency, control over system resources, and rich ecosystem of libraries.

1.2. Challenges Faced

- **Complexity of Graphics Rendering**: Achieving high-quality graphics required advanced rendering techniques, which could strain CPU and GPU resources.
- **Real-Time Physics Calculations**: The game engine needed to simulate realistic physics in real-time, necessitating efficient algorithms and data structures.
- **Cross-Platform Support**: The engine had to run on multiple platforms, including consoles, PCs, and mobile devices, requiring careful management of platform-specific code.

1.3. Strategies Employed

- **Modular Architecture**: The development team adopted a modular architecture, separating the rendering engine, physics engine, and input management into distinct modules. This approach facilitated easier updates and maintenance.
- **Utilization of Existing Libraries**: The team leveraged libraries such as OpenGL for rendering and Bullet Physics for physics simulation, allowing them to focus on the game engine's core features.
- **Optimized Resource Management**: To ensure performance, the team implemented object pooling for frequently created and destroyed objects, minimizing dynamic memory allocations during gameplay.

1.4. Outcomes

The game engine was successfully developed and used in multiple high-profile games, achieving:

- **High Frame Rates**: The engine provided smooth gameplay at high frame rates across various hardware configurations.
- **Realistic Physics Simulations**: Players experienced immersive game-

play with realistic physics interactions.

- **Scalability**: The modular architecture allowed the team to easily extend the engine with new features and optimizations in future game releases.

2. Case Study 2: Cloud-Based Video Processing Platform

2.1. Overview

A startup focused on creating a cloud-based video processing platform that allows users to upload, process, and stream videos seamlessly. The platform aimed to provide high-quality video transcoding and real-time editing capabilities using C++ for its performance and efficiency.

2.2. Challenges Faced

- **Handling Large Video Files**: The platform needed to efficiently handle large video files and perform transcoding operations without significant delays.
- **Concurrency and Scalability**: With many users uploading videos simultaneously, the system required robust concurrency management to prevent bottlenecks.
- **Cost Management**: As a cloud service, optimizing resource usage was crucial to minimize operational costs while maintaining performance.

2.3. Strategies Employed

- **Efficient Codec Implementations**: The team implemented optimized codecs in C++ to ensure rapid video processing and transcoding, utilizing SIMD (Single Instruction, Multiple Data) for performance boosts.
- **Asynchronous Processing**: By using asynchronous I/O and worker threads, the platform could process multiple video files concurrently, improving responsiveness and throughput.
- **Cloud Resource Optimization**: The team utilized cloud provider features such as auto-scaling and load balancing to ensure efficient resource usage and scalability during peak loads.

2.4. Outcomes

The cloud-based video processing platform gained traction, achieving:

- **Rapid Processing Times**: Users reported significantly reduced video processing times, leading to higher satisfaction and engagement.
- **Scalability**: The platform successfully handled increased workloads during peak usage, maintaining performance without additional infrastructure costs.
- **Market Growth**: The startup attracted new customers, expanding its service offerings to include live streaming and advanced video analytics.

3. Case Study 3: Financial Trading System

3.1. Overview

A financial services firm developed a high-frequency trading (HFT) application to execute trades at lightning speed. The choice of C++ was driven by the need for performance, low latency, and direct access to system resources.

3.2. Challenges Faced

- **Low Latency Requirements**: In HFT, even microseconds matter. The system needed to minimize latency at every level.
- **Concurrency Issues**: Managing concurrent operations in a multi-threaded environment posed challenges related to data consistency and synchronization.
- **Regulatory Compliance**: The system had to comply with financial regulations regarding data security and transaction integrity.

3.3. Strategies Employed

- **Optimized Data Structures**: The team implemented specialized data structures to handle market data and orders efficiently, minimizing access times.

- **Lock-Free Programming**: To reduce contention in multi-threaded operations, the team employed lock-free programming techniques, which improved throughput and reduced latency.
- **Rigorous Testing**: The development process included extensive testing, including performance profiling and stress testing, to ensure the system could handle extreme loads and maintain low latency.

3.4. Outcomes

The HFT application became a key component of the firm's trading strategy, achieving:

- **Market Leadership**: The application allowed the firm to compete effectively in the fast-paced financial market, consistently executing trades ahead of competitors.
- **High Throughput**: The system handled thousands of transactions per second with minimal latency, enabling rapid responses to market changes.
- **Regulatory Compliance**: The firm maintained compliance with financial regulations, ensuring the integrity and security of its trading operations.

4. Case Study 4: Real-Time Data Analytics Platform

4.1. Overview

A technology company aimed to create a real-time data analytics platform that processes streaming data from various sources, including IoT devices and web applications. C++ was chosen for its performance and ability to handle high data throughput.

4.2. Challenges Faced

- **High Volume Data Processing**: The platform needed to process and analyze large volumes of data in real-time without lag.
- **Data Integration from Multiple Sources**: The ability to ingest data

from various sources in different formats posed integration challenges.

- **Fault Tolerance**: Ensuring the system could recover gracefully from failures was critical for maintaining data integrity.

4.3. Strategies Employed

- **Stream Processing Framework**: The team implemented a stream processing framework in C++ that allowed for real-time data ingestion and processing.
- **Data Partitioning**: By partitioning data streams, the platform could distribute the processing load across multiple nodes, improving scalability.
- **Checkpointing Mechanisms**: To ensure fault tolerance, the team implemented checkpointing, allowing the system to recover to a consistent state in case of failures.

4.4. Outcomes

The real-time data analytics platform was successfully deployed, achieving:

- **Real-Time Insights**: Users gained the ability to access real-time insights from their data, enhancing decision-making capabilities.
- **Scalability**: The platform efficiently scaled to handle increasing data volumes without degradation in performance.
- **Robustness**: The implementation of fault tolerance mechanisms ensured high availability and reliability, even under adverse conditions.

5. Case Study 5: Cross-Platform Desktop Application

5.1. Overview

A software development company sought to create a cross-platform desktop application for project management. The application needed to run seamlessly on Windows, macOS, and Linux, leveraging C++ for performance and portability.

5.2. Challenges Faced

- **Cross-Platform Compatibility**: Ensuring consistent functionality and appearance across different operating systems was a significant challenge.
- **User Interface Design**: Creating a user-friendly interface that adheres to the design guidelines of each platform required careful planning.
- **Performance Optimization**: The application needed to handle large project datasets efficiently without performance degradation.

5.3. Strategies Employed

- **Qt Framework**: The team utilized the Qt framework to build the application, allowing for consistent cross-platform development while leveraging C++'s performance.
- **Conditional Compilation**: The codebase included conditional compilation directives to manage platform-specific functionality without cluttering the code.
- **User-Centric Design**: Extensive user testing was conducted to ensure the interface was intuitive and aligned with users' expectations on each platform.

5.4. Outcomes

The project management application was successfully launched, achieving:

- **Wide Adoption**: The application gained a large user base across different operating systems, thanks to its cross-platform capabilities.
- **Consistent User Experience**: Users reported a seamless experience regardless of the platform, enhancing productivity and satisfaction.
- **Scalable Architecture**: The application's architecture allowed for easy addition of new features and enhancements based on user feedback.

6. Lessons Learned from C++ Development Case Studies

6.1. Importance of Performance Optimization

Across all case studies, performance optimization emerged as a critical factor in the success of C++ applications. Developers should prioritize performance at every stage of development, from architecture to implementation.

6.2. Modular Design Principles

Modular design allows for better maintainability, testing, and scalability. By breaking applications into distinct components, teams can work concurrently and manage complexity more effectively.

6.3. Thorough Testing Practices

Rigorous testing is essential to ensure software reliability and performance. Incorporating automated testing, profiling, and user feedback throughout the development lifecycle leads to higher-quality applications.

6.4. Adaptability and Continuous Learning

The software development landscape is constantly evolving. Developers must remain adaptable, continuously learning and incorporating new technologies and best practices to stay competitive.

Conclusion

In this chapter, we explored several real-world case studies that highlight the successful application of C++ in various domains, from gaming to finance and cloud computing. Each case study illustrated the challenges faced, strategies employed, and outcomes achieved, providing valuable insights into best practices in C++ development. The lessons learned from these experiences emphasize the importance of performance optimization, modular design, thorough testing, and continuous learning. As C++ continues to evolve, these principles will remain critical for developing scalable and high-quality software solutions.

Chapter 15: The Future of C++: Trends, Innovations, and Opportunities

Introduction

C++ has been a cornerstone of systems programming and high-performance applications for decades. As technology evolves, the language continues to adapt, incorporating new features and paradigms that enhance its capabilities. This chapter explores the future of C++, focusing on emerging trends, innovations in the language, and the opportunities these developments present for developers. By examining the evolving landscape of software development, we can understand how C++ remains relevant and powerful in addressing contemporary challenges.

1. The Evolution of C++

1.1. Historical Context

C++ was developed in the early 1980s by Bjarne Stroustrup as an enhancement to the C programming language. It introduced object-oriented features while maintaining the efficiency and performance characteristics of C. Over the years, C++ has undergone several iterations, each adding new features and paradigms, including:

- **C++98**: The first standardized version of C++, introducing templates, exceptions, and the Standard Template Library (STL).
- **C++11**: A significant update that introduced features like auto keyword, range-based for loops, lambda expressions, and smart pointers.
- **C++14 and C++17**: Smaller updates that refined existing features and introduced new ones, such as std::optional and std::variant.
- **C++20**: A major revision that introduced concepts, coroutines, and modules, significantly enhancing the language's capabilities.

1.2. Current State of C++

As of now, C++ remains one of the most widely used programming languages, especially in systems programming, game development, embedded systems, and high-performance computing. Its rich feature set and efficiency make it a preferred choice for applications where performance is critical.

2. Emerging Trends in C++ Development

2.1. Increased Adoption of Modern C++ Features

Developers are increasingly adopting modern C++ features introduced in C++11 and beyond. Features such as auto keyword, smart pointers, and lambda expressions simplify code and enhance safety.

- **Best Practices**: Emphasizing the use of modern features promotes writing safer and more maintainable code, reducing the risk of memory leaks and undefined behavior.

2.2. Growth of C++ in Data Science and Machine Learning

C++ is gaining traction in data science and machine learning due to its performance capabilities. Libraries like TensorFlow and PyTorch have C++ APIs, allowing developers to implement high-performance machine learning models.

- **Opportunities**: C++ developers can leverage their skills to enter the growing fields of AI and data science, which increasingly require efficient and performant solutions.

2.3. Integration with Other Languages

C++ is often used alongside other programming languages, such as Python and Java, to take advantage of its performance characteristics. This trend is seen in areas like:

- **Python Bindings**: Many libraries, such as Boost.Python, enable C++ code to be called from Python, combining the ease of Python with the performance of C++.

2.4. Cloud Computing and C++

As cloud computing becomes ubiquitous, C++ is being used in developing cloud-native applications. Its performance and resource management capabilities make it suitable for high-performance services running in the cloud.

- **Trends**: The demand for cloud services will drive the need for C++ developers who can build efficient, scalable applications.

3. Innovations in the C++ Language

3.1. C++23 Features and Expectations

C++23 is expected to introduce several features that enhance the language's capabilities:

- **Pattern Matching**: This feature aims to simplify complex data handling by allowing developers to match data structures against patterns, improving code clarity.
- **Static Reflection**: Static reflection will enable developers to introspect and manipulate types at compile time, enhancing metaprogramming capabilities.

- **Enhanced Ranges**: Improvements to the ranges library will provide developers with more powerful tools for working with sequences of data.

3.2. Continued Standardization Efforts

The C++ standards committee is actively working on future iterations of the language. Developers can expect ongoing improvements and additions to the language, driven by community feedback and industry needs.

- **Community Involvement**: Engaging with the C++ community through forums, conferences, and working groups can influence the future direction of the language.

4. C++ in the Context of Emerging Technologies

4.1. The Role of C++ in IoT

The Internet of Things (IoT) continues to grow, and C++ is well-positioned to support the development of IoT applications due to its efficiency and performance.

- **Challenges in IoT Development**: C++ developers will face challenges related to resource constraints, real-time processing, and security in IoT devices.
- **Opportunities**: Building efficient C++ applications for IoT can lead to innovations in smart home devices, industrial automation, and connected vehicles.

4.2. C++ and Quantum Computing

As quantum computing emerges, C++ could play a vital role in developing software that interacts with quantum systems.

- **Potential Libraries**: Future libraries may enable C++ to interact with quantum computing frameworks, allowing developers to explore new computing paradigms.

4.3. C++ for High-Performance Computing (HPC)

C++ remains a staple in high-performance computing applications. The demand for computational power in scientific research, simulations, and data analysis continues to grow.

- **Trends in HPC**: With the rise of exascale computing, C++ developers will need to focus on optimizing code for parallel execution and leveraging advancements in hardware.

5. Opportunities for C++ Developers

5.1. Career Growth in C++

As C++ continues to evolve and adapt to new technologies, the demand for skilled C++ developers remains high. Opportunities exist in various industries, including:

- **Game Development**: The gaming industry continues to grow, with a constant need for high-performance engines and applications.
- **Finance**: The financial sector requires robust and efficient software for trading systems and analytics.
- **Embedded Systems**: C++ is widely used in developing embedded systems, which are integral to automotive, aerospace, and consumer electronics industries.

5.2. Expanding Skill Sets

C++ developers should consider expanding their skill sets to include complementary technologies and paradigms:

- **Learning New Libraries and Frameworks**: Familiarity with libraries like Boost, Qt, and machine learning frameworks can enhance a developer's capabilities.
- **Exploring Other Languages**: Knowledge of languages like Python, Rust, or Go can provide a competitive edge and enable more versatile

development.

5.3. Community Engagement and Contribution

Engaging with the C++ community through open-source contributions, forums, and conferences can lead to personal and professional growth.

- **Open Source Projects**: Contributing to open-source C++ projects allows developers to learn from others, improve their skills, and gain recognition within the community.

6. Challenges Ahead for C++ Development

6.1. Learning Curve and Complexity

While C++ offers significant advantages, it also presents a steep learning curve, particularly for new developers. The complexity of the language and its paradigms can be daunting.

- **Addressing the Learning Curve**: Educational resources, tutorials, and community support can help new developers overcome these challenges.

6.2. Competition from Higher-Level Languages

Languages like Python and JavaScript offer ease of use and rapid development capabilities, posing competition to C++ in some domains.

- **Positioning C++**: C++ can maintain its position by emphasizing performance, efficiency, and the ability to interface with low-level systems.

7. Real-World Examples of C++ Innovations

7.1. Case Study 1: Autonomous Vehicles

Examine how C++ is utilized in the development of autonomous vehicle systems, focusing on real-time data processing, sensor integration, and control systems.

- **Technological Advancements**: Discuss the integration of machine learning and computer vision with C++ for advanced driving features.

7.2. Case Study 2: Medical Imaging Systems

Analyze the role of C++ in developing medical imaging software, high-lighting its performance in processing large datasets and ensuring real-time imaging capabilities.

- **Impact on Healthcare**: Emphasize how innovations in imaging technology enhance diagnostic capabilities and patient outcomes.

7.3. Case Study 3: Virtual Reality Applications

Explore how C++ is used in creating immersive virtual reality experiences, focusing on performance optimizations and real-time rendering techniques.

- **Future of Gaming and Entertainment**: Discuss the implications of VR technology on the entertainment industry and user experience.

8. Conclusion

The future of C++ development is bright, with numerous opportunities and innovations on the horizon. As the language evolves, developers must adapt to new features, embrace emerging trends, and remain engaged with the community. By leveraging the strengths of C++, particularly in performance and efficiency, developers can build scalable applications that meet the demands of a rapidly changing technological landscape. The case studies presented illustrate the real-world impact of C++ and provide a glimpse into its potential for future growth and innovation. As we move forward, the insights gained from this chapter will serve as a valuable guide for navigating the exciting future of C++ development.

Conclusion

As we reach the end of our exploration into C++ development and scalability, it becomes clear that C++ remains a vital and dynamic force in the landscape of software engineering. From its origins as a systems programming language to its current applications in high-performance computing, game development, cloud services, and artificial intelligence, C++ continues to adapt and evolve, meeting the demands of modern technology.

Throughout this book, we have delved into various facets of C++ development, emphasizing its strengths in performance, efficiency, and flexibility. We have explored the intricacies of the language, highlighting its robust features and powerful capabilities that enable developers to build scalable and high-performance applications.

Key Themes Explored

Scalability as a Core Principle: One of the overarching themes of this book has been the emphasis on scalability in software design. As applications grow in complexity and user demand, the need for scalable architectures becomes paramount. C++ provides the tools and methodologies necessary to create systems that can scale efficiently, whether through modular design, optimized resource management, or effective concurrency techniques.

Modern C++ Features: With each iteration of the C++ standard, new features have emerged that enhance the language's usability and safety. From the introduction of smart pointers in C++11 to the exciting possibilities of modules and concepts in C++20, modern C++ is designed to help developers write cleaner, safer, and more efficient code. Embracing these features is crucial for developers looking to leverage the full power of the language.

Performance Optimization: C++ is synonymous with performance, and the techniques for optimizing applications have been thoroughly discussed. Profiling tools, resource management strategies, and algorithmic improvements are essential skills for any C++ developer. As we move towards a future that demands more from our applications, understanding how to optimize performance will remain a critical competency.

Cross-Platform Development: The ability to develop cross-platform applications is increasingly important in a diverse technological landscape. C++'s rich ecosystem of libraries and frameworks enables developers to build applications that run seamlessly on various operating systems. By managing platform-specific code and leveraging modern build systems, C++ developers can create robust applications that cater to a broad audience.

Emerging Technologies and Future Trends: As we have explored in the final chapters, the future of C++ is bright. The language is poised to play a significant role in emerging technologies, such as artificial intelligence, machine learning, and cloud computing. With its performance advantages and ability to interface with hardware, C++ will continue to be a preferred choice for developers looking to build innovative solutions.

The Road Ahead

The journey of mastering C++ is ongoing. As technology evolves, so too will the tools, practices, and methodologies associated with C++ development. For current and aspiring developers, it is essential to stay engaged with the C++ community, continuously learn, and adapt to new trends and innovations. This includes participating in forums, attending conferences, and contributing to open-source projects to not only enhance personal skills but also to help shape the future of C++.

Final Thoughts

In closing, C++ is more than just a programming language; it is a powerful tool for solving complex problems and building the next generation of software applications. Whether you are developing high-performance systems, creating interactive games, or designing scalable cloud services, the principles, practices, and insights shared in this book will serve as a solid foundation for your C++ development endeavors.

As you move forward in your journey, embrace the challenges and opportunities that come with using C++. By leveraging its strengths, adhering to best practices, and remaining open to innovation, you can contribute to the exciting future of C++ and the broader field of software development. The road ahead is filled with possibilities, and the skills you cultivate in C++

will empower you to navigate this landscape effectively.

Thank you for embarking on this journey through C++ development and scalability. May your future projects be successful, your code be clean, and your applications be scalable!

www.ingramcontent.com/pod-product-compliance
Lightning Source LLC
Chambersburg PA
CBHW071002050326
40689CB00014B/3454